a novel by

C.H. Green

Thank you for your love & support through the journey!

C H Green

From
Pharaoh's
Hand

FROM PHARAOH'S HAND

--A Prodigal in the Wilderness

Dedicated to my wonderful son who helped me brainstorm, who is and always will be the sunshine of my life.

Copyright 2013 All rights reserved.

ISBN: 9781304047564

All rights reserved. No part of this book may be used or reproduced in any manner whatsoever without written permission, except in the case of brief quotations embodied in critical articles and reviews, without written permission from the publisher. The characters and events in this book are fictitious. Any similarity to a real person, living or dead, is coincidental and not intended by the author.

Chapter 1

"Thou shalt not kill."

It was well after midnight when the SUV pulled back into the back parking lot of a boarded up motel and cut its lights. The mission had been a success. Frankie had promised to pay Catfish extra if he would help with this one heist. All Catfish would have to do was watch out for the security guard making his rounds. It was even better and easier than he thought it would be. And what a haul they had made.

"Look at all this gold, would you. Man, must be a fortune here. What do ya suppose this is, Bones?" Frankie asked Catfish as he pulled a heavy odd shaped item resembling a crocodile from the pillowcase.

"Probably one of them idols that heathen worship. Is it heavy? I bet it's solid gold."

"Yeah, man. It's heavy. Here, hold it and see. And look here in this fancy box all   trimmed in gold. Ain't it cool, man? There's rings. Five of 'em. All of them solid too, I bet ya. Here's

2

this plate with the funny writing. Oh here's the translation down at the bottom: 'Death to all who enter Pharaoh's tomb.'" His eyes widened in mock horror. "whoa, scary stuff. Good thing I ain't superstitious. I sho ain't. These babies going ta change my luck forever." And he whistled a low whistle of admiration.

"Well, now Frankie, helping you pull off this here elaborate job, it bein' so risky an' all, well I figure a special reward on top o' my standard rate. Whadda ya say?"

"What exactly did you have in mind? You know I don't get paid on the goods 'til they delivered to Ace."

"Well, what Ace don't know won't hurt him. How about one of them there gold rings plus my five grand."

"Naw, man. All you did was watch the hallway. I took all the heat."

"Whadda ya mean… I could have been shot to death back there!"

"Wouldn't be no big loss. Besides, what's a stupid redneck like you gonna do with a gold ring? You low-class white trash moocher," said Frankie, throwing his head back for a big belly laugh. The laughter ended, though, when the idol came crashing down against his bare head.

"You low-down thievin' Memphis mafia scum! Nobody calls Phineas Catfish Jones stupid. Nobody!"

The idol came down on Frankie's skull three times more. The second blow had already rendered him unconscious, but Catfish was so infuriated at Frankie's attempt to cheat him out of payment that he just kept striking. Blood poured from Frankie's head. Who was this low belly calling a redneck? Bones had risked his life, just like Frankie.

Cat labored to breathe when he finally stopped to survey the damage to Frankie. Once again his temper had won. If he had just been patient. If he had just let Frankie have his laugh, he could have convinced him that he deserved the reward. But Frankie was gone now. There was no sign of life. Catfish held the bloody idol in his hand and wondered what in tarnation he was going to do next.

The river. The river was his answer. It was not that far away. He could drive Frankie's SUV to the river, put it in gear, and let it sink to the bottom of the muddy Mississippi. Frankie would never be heard from again. Catfish regretted that the golden idol would have to go too. It had his fingerprints all over it, not to mention all that blood. *One couldn't be too careful these days, what with all them fancy pants scientists and their DNA.*

"Cryin' shame. Bet that was worth a pretty penny," he said aloud.

But at least he had the rings and the fancy box.

Catfish got out on the passenger side, checked to make sure they were safe from view, and pulled Frankie's lifeless body over to the passenger side. What a mess. *Frankie, my man, you shoulda never try to con a country boy.* He fumbled around in Frankie's vest pocket and found his wallet. *Serves you right. Now I get my five grand plus what you got left, not to mention these here golden trinkets.* He stuffed the wad of bills down in his pants pocket and started the SUV. Good thing the river wasn't far. He would have to walk back to the truck. And walking around this part of the city this time of night gave him the creeps. No telling what danger lurked around the alleyways and tall dark buildings. There just was no telling.

5

Chapter 2
Hiding the Evidence

'Behold I show you a mystery; we shall not all sleep...'   *1 Corinthians 15:51*

Everything had gone as well as expected, she reckoned. She

hadn't been missed yet. No one was the wiser. Elizabeth had

swapped the gym clothes in her backpack for the clothes and

money she had stashed in her car. She had worked her regular four

hours and then hopped the casino shuttle at the end of Wal-Mart

parking lot around 7 p.m. Piece of cake. Throwing back the covers,

she sat up in bed too fast and the room swam. She decided it might

be best to just sit still for a few moments for it to pass, and as she did so, reflected on the long night that had just passed.

Two silver haired ladies had passed the time on the bus ride discussing the seafood buffet at the Grand Hotel, and the eighty miles ticked off quickly as they passed by the Brownsville and Somerville exits. Billboard after billboard promoted the loosest slots in Tunica or the stage shows at the Horseshoe, the litany of casino advertisements being broken by one that was particularly colorful. "King Tut is back," It featured a huge golden head of the ancient Pharaoh. Other than that, there had not been much to see en route to Memphis on I-40, except the occasional State Trooper or stalled vehicle by the side of the road.

Elizabeth had told the driver she was sick and needed a rest area once they reached the outskirts of town, but just as she had mustered the courage to begin her scene, a gentleman near the front had spoken up.

"I believe my lady friend here would like to shop a bit before we proceed to drop our nest egg down the slots. Anyone else feel like stretching their legs?"

"Hey, that's a good idea. I hear that new Wolfchase mall has an ice cream parlor."

"What do you say, Ralph, can we make a pit stop?"

"Don't matter to me none," said the driver. "I get paid the same either way, buddy.

"Well you just passed the exit," muttered another near the front of the shuttle.

"It's okay. I can take Exit 15 and double back. I need to fill up too."

Elizabeth had ditched the party at the Shell station. It was no big deal. Finding her way around Memphis--that was going to be the big deal. She wished she had taken the time to print out directions.

She had been shopping in Memphis many times with her parents. She had seen most of the landmarks like Graceland, Sun Records, and Beale Street, and she had gone to sporting events at the dazzling replica of the Pyramid. She had been on field trips to the Pink Palace museum and the Memphis Zoo. But her parents had always driven while she slept in the backseat, or she was busy chatting with friends on the bus. She was fairly clueless about how to get anywhere in a city this size. It was a good thing she had purchased a map of Memphis back at the convenience store. That and a Diet Dr. Pepper.

Her first priority had been to find a hotel for the night, but she needed a phone book. How sick and anxious she had been, as she had waited in line behind a well-dressed, clean-cut black man of about fifty sporting a huge diamond ring and new leather loafers. Behind him was a not-so-well-dressed, thin white man with a scraggly beard and holes in his faded grungy jeans. He appeared to be in his forties, though with all the facial hair, Beth wasn't real sure. They had bought Marlboros and Miller Lite and seemed to know each other. Elizabeth remembered how she had thumbed through a Hollywood tabloid near the counter trying to hide the fact that she was eavesdropping.

"You wanna follow me so you'll know where you're going?" the black man asked.

"Yep. I'll be right behind you. Don't git too far ahead a me now."

"Now how'm I gonna lose that big old rattletrap you drive. Man, ain't it time for some new wheels?"

"I'm workin on it. A couple more jobs ought to get me into a Navigator."

"Yeah, man. Then you be stylin and profilin and all yo buddies be wondering where you get the jack to afford all that."

The dirty white man's grin revealed several crooked, yellowed teeth with a large gap in the bottom. Beth remembered recoiling in disgust at the smell of stale smoke, body odor, and garlic. The man's nicotine-stained fingers fidgeted with a ring of keys as he spoke.

"Don't you worry 'bout that. I'll keep Old Faithful for 'round town and drive the Navigator when I make my trips into the city. Gonna finally get me a decent roof over my head too."

"I hear ya Bones. I hear ya."

Track buddies? Maybe. Southland Greyhound park was just west of Memphis across the river bridge. She had known that much. She guessed the dirty white man had won a couple of thousand and was dreaming to hit it big on his next gambling excursion. *He probably has a wife ana six children at home,* she remembered thinking to herself as the two men headed out the door. She had stood there for a moment and watched as the man called Bones went to the back of his rusted out, two-toned, black and red GMC, placed the beer inside, then hoisted what appeared to be a 100 lb. bag of feed onto his shoulder. The black man opened the back door of his SUV, and the bag was thrown inside. The two shook hands, looked around, and then looked directly toward her. She looked both ways and pretended she was looking for a cab or someone to pick her up and then took the phone book back to the booth and slid onto the cracked red seat to plot her course.

Maybe the guy has horses, she had shrugged, but there had been more important concerns to attend to for the night.

She had searched for the abortion clinic in the Yellow Pages. There might be even more than one. She wanted a clinic that would ask no questions and that would take cash, although she had no idea what it might cost. She hoped she had enough. By this time tomorrow she would be headed home. Being alone in the big city made her nervous, but she had her cell phone and money. Surely she could make it one night.

As she stepped out onto the oily parking lot, her stomach had churned at the smell of the gas fumes emitted by a running car nearby. *I'm just seventeen.* She kept pushing the tales of botched abortions from her mind. She convinced herself that this was

11

twenty-first century. It would all be fine. Within twenty-four hours all her worries would be over.

She had paid cash for a room at the Wingate with a double bed and a view of the Interstate. The clerk had asked no questions other than for a credit card for incidentals. Elizabeth hesitated, and then pulled out the MasterCard and passed it to the clerk without a word. The clerk had simply noted the expiration date on the card and other details and handed it back to her. That was all there was to it. If there were no charges on the card, it wouldn't matter anyhow.

"Thank you. We hope you enjoy your stay in Memphis."

It had been easier than she ever thought it would be. Once inside room 314, Elizabeth had pulled back the burgundy coverlet on the bed and checked for clean sheets. That was the first thing her mother always did when they went on vacation. Satisfied, she had sat on the edge of the bed, turned the television on, and wondered how things were at home. That had been around 9 p.m. If everything went as planned, her parents would have no reason to check on her. She had never given them reason to doubt her before, and Crystal wouldn't dare squeal on her. She had too much dirt on

Crystal for that to happen.

Maybe she should have called Crystal. She was supposed to be with her boyfriend Chris, at least that's what she told Crystal. He had suggested her staying overnight before, in fact, but she had always turned him down. It was too risky, but now it seemed like the perfect alibi.

"You're actually going to spend the night?" Crystal had asked incredulously. "Won't his parents know? How are you going to pull that off?"

"I'll sneak in through the basement. We'll crash down there, wake up and leave before his parents get up. Maybe leave them a note that he's picking me up and spending the day with me...shopping, lunch, bowling alley, that sort of thing. They will never know."

"I hope you're right. If you chicken out, just call me. You can crash here."

"It's our secret. Pinky swear."

Elizabeth frowned as she remembered the fib. Lying to her best friend since kindergarten, how low could she get? But Crystal might tell her parents. She was in this alone. It would be her secret

13

forever. She thought back to last fall and how all her troubles began. If she could just go back to that night and say no, everything would be okay. Why hadn't she just said no?

That was the night the North Side Indians had won their first and last game of the season 41 to 38. She closed her eyes, and she could see the elated team as it ran from the field and celebrated their win over the Lexington Tigers. The band danced from side to side as they blasted out their victory song. Coach Fry, drenched with ice water, was laughing from the sidelines. Players slapped each other's behinds and hugged. A sea of blue and gold uniforms cheered and bobbed with adrenaline. Elizabeth jumped into her new boyfriend's arms and kissed him. It felt good to win at least their Homecoming game.

"We did it!" he puffed breathlessly. Chris Daily had just run fifty yards to make the winning touchdown.

"No, you did it, Chris. You did it."

"Let's go celebrate."

She had been with Chris since the beginning of the school year, and it still made her smile that all her girlfriends envied her. Elizabeth had mustered the courage to ask him to the Fall Festival dance. And of course he had said yes, because Elizabeth Morgan Merriweather--with her winning smile, golden hair, and model figure--had no trouble crooking her finger and getting what she wanted. "We are the perfect couple," she had said to Crystal. And Crystal had agreed, because that's what best friends do.

The Band Boosters had organized the Homecoming Party in the gymnasium, but everyone knew that party was for the nerds and geeks. The real party was at the Country Club, and only Jackson's most elite were invited to attend. The very affluent families of Madison County sent their children to private schools like University School on the west side of town. But there were snobs in the public system as well. Each system had its own hierarchy.

Chris and Elizabeth had made their required appearance in the gymnasium and were heading over to the main event in his souped-up, red-lacquered, convertible Mustang on this mild late autumn evening in November. Elizabeth thought she looked very grown up in her black leather mini and knee-high boots, and despite the warmth of the season, the two were sitting so close that Elizabeth could steer if she had wanted.

"How about we make a grand entrance in just a little while? Feel like a drive in the country?" he had said. Beth had shrugged and agreed to whatever Chris wanted. She was eager to please and lived for his smile.

Chris made a right at the light. He made a left onto Oil Well Drive and took it all the way out to Highway 412 west. Within ten more minutes, they had left the lights of Jackson, Tennessee behind and were headed out toward a rural community that the locals called Windy City. They made a right onto Windy City Road and followed it a few more miles until they came to a gravel road on the right. The road sign read "Bascomb Road" and was crooked from a botched attempt at theft. The stop sign beneath it was spray-painted with an expletive. Chris followed the gravel road about a quarter of a mile and cut the engine and lights. From here there were no city lights to dim the autumn stars above. Here there were no chaperones or curious eyes. Her cheeks were flush with excitement.

"How did you know about this road?" Elizabeth asked.

"We ride our four-wheelers out here in the summer time. We're not far from the house. It's just over there through the trees.

In daytime, you can see the roof of my house."

"I'm surprised you haven't brought me here before."

"I haven't brought anyone here. I was waiting for the perfect girl and the perfect time."

Elizabeth's breath had caught, and her heart had begun thumping hard in her chest. Even though she was one of the most popular girls in school, she still struggled with low self-esteem. She lived to please people, to make them adore her--craving the attention that both admiring friends and doting relatives gave. Elizabeth was the one who always volunteered to tutor after class, the one who headed up the fundraisers for charity and spent countless hours grading papers for her favorite teacher, even though it bothered her to be branded a teacher's pet. "No" was not in her vocabulary. *He thinks I'm special...the perfect girl.*

She remembered his hand moving to caress her face. With one finger he had traced her forehead, her brow, her cheekbone, and then moved to her ear. She could almost feel his touch again tonight. She had closed her eyes and let his touch send shivers through her. She remembered his cologne and the way his hair fell over one eye, and that grin. That dimpled grin he had as he trailed

17

his finger down her neck. Her eyes were closed, but she knew he was going to kiss her. All her shyness had left her, as they experimented with kissing. So this was what all the fuss was about. Kissing, kissing, laughing, kissing. His left hand was traveling up her leg toward the hem of her leather skirt. She giggled and tried to push his hand away. *He loves me. He really does love me. He brought me here to this special place. It will be our special place from now on.*

"Beth?"

"Uh huh…"

"You want to?"

"Uh huh.

"You sure?"

Beth hesitated. *No, I'm not sure. I'm not sure I'm ready for this. I can't… what would my parents say if they found out?*

'Well…I…uh…"

"It's okay. If you're gonna be a baby about it…"

"Uh…no, no. It's fine. It's fine. I want to."

He needed no other permission. In seconds the passenger seat was laid back, and she was letting Chris have his way. She seemed a little shell shocked, as he rolled back to his side of the car

18

after a short time. She remembered thinking, *What's wrong? Dia 1 do it wrong?*

"It's okay. Everyone knows you can't get pregnant the first time. That was your first time, wasn't it?"

She blushed. "Yes."

"I thought so. Did I hurt you?"

"No, it's okay. I love you Chris."

"Love you too Baby. We better get to the Country Club, or they will be looking for us."

"Right," she mumbled as she put herself back together; she hadn't even removed her skirt. She could not stop grinning as she pulled her best friend, Crystal Barnes into the girls' restroom.

"You did what?"

"We did it in his car. On Bascomb Road."

Crystal giggled.

"No way. Are you serious? You're kidding, right? Did it hurt?"

"Yeah, a little. But I didn't let on."

"Oh my gosh, I can't believe it."

If Crystal haa trouble believing that, she woula never believe what was going on now. If she coula just turn back time. If she haa just saia no, she wouldn't be

19

in this crummy hotel with this awful need to throw up every hour.

Weeks later, Chris had talked her into trying some bourbon he had snuck from his dad's liquor cabinet. Before she knew it two hours had passed, and the bottle lay empty on the floor beside them. She remembered she could not stop laughing. *How could I have been so stupid?*

After that incident was when Beth had decided to go to an out of the way convenience store where no one would know her. She slid the pregnancy test into her buggy beneath a huge box of pads. She was late, but she was still hopeful. She checked to make sure the lady at the counter was not someone she knew, then made her way to the counter with her purchases, a bag of chips, a drink, and some Skittles thrown in. The clerk raised an eyebrow but did not comment as Beth grabbed the sacks and hurried home to take the test before her parents got off work.

Half an hour later, she had sat on the toilet and cried as the double pink lines appeared. Could it be a faulty test? She took the other stick from the package and repeated the two-minute process. In no time, the double pink lines appeared again. This time, there was no doubt, only dismay, and then hysteria.

20

How could I have done this? How can this be? How can I disappoint Mom and Dad? I'm supposed to go to college and become an accountant. Oh no. What have I done? Chris. She had to tell Chris. No, she could not tell Chris. He had a full scholarship to the University of Tennessee. He was going to be a professional football player. *My life is over.*

All Elizabeth could think was how mad her parents would be. An unwanted teen pregnancy would ruin her father's chance at any political career. Her mother would be the social outcast of the Club. She would be shunned at school -- if she got to finish school. She counted the months.

It had to have been the first time. That was in late November. It was late January now, so...I could still graduate, but I'll be six months along by then, and there'd be no hiding it. By the time August rolls around when I should be starting college at Union, the baby will be here. It was all she could do to keep from hyperventilating. *If I tell Chris, will he marry me? I can't ask him to give up his pro football career to work late nights delivering pizzas. I just can't.*

She had heard of girls getting in trouble like this. Their parents took them to have the baby aborted in Memphis or Nashville. They would be gone from school for a week or so, saying

21

they had mono or the flu. But everyone talked just the same. Especially if the girl had told all her girlfriends she had been sleeping with her boyfriend. *I'm glad I only told Crystal. But who had Chris told? Think Beth. Think.*

That's when she had decided she could go to Memphis on her own and get it done. But she had just got her license, and driving in Jackson was nerve-wracking, much less driving in a big city like Memphis. *Who could I trust to take me? I don't want anyone to know. Not even Crystal. I could ride a Greyhound. No, I can't do that either. I don't want to go downtown by myself. It's dangerous in that part of town.* Beth remembered burying her head in her hands and sobbing. *Chris was right. I am a baby. A baby having a baby.* She lay her head over on the cool ceramic countertop and tried to figure a way out of her predicament. *If I didn't have to work Friday night, I could leave school early and ...hey wait.*

That might work, she had thought as she sat up. She saw the bus leaving almost every Friday evening when she got off her part-time job at Wal-mart. Money wasn't a problem. She had money she had been saving to get a new laptop. Being gone overnight would be the problem. She would go to the clinic

22

Saturday, get it done and be home by Saturday night. She could ask Crystal to cover for her, and tell her that she would be at Chris's. *I'm going to have to lie to my very best friend. Can I do that? And will she believe me? I don't know if I can do this. I have to. I have no choice. There's no way out of this mess but to go through with it.* It was going to be a long week of waiting and planning. *Maybe it was just a fluke,* she told herself. *I can't be pregnant. You don't get pregnant the first time ...Do you?*

Well, Chris had been wrong about that, Beth had thought sadly as she had lain there on the hotel bed last night, in a cheap Memphis hotel room, desperate, despondent, and sick with the TV blaring. She had not been paying much attention to the television, but soft, kind words began to break through. "Adrian Rogers, pastor of Bellevue Baptist," the marquee at the bottom of the screen said. That was the huge church she had seen from the shuttle as they crossed the Interstate. The tall crosses that lit the night sky had caught her attention. She could throw a rock and hit it from here. Well, not quite. But it was just across the field. He had preached about faith:

"By faith Moses, when he was born, was hid three months of his parents, because they saw he was a proper child; and they were not afraid of the king's commandment," he quoted. "The life we live on this earth is lived by faith. Through the grace of God we are saved. Ephesians 2:8-9 says: 'For by grace are ye saved through faith; and that not of yourselves: it is the gift of God'. His love and mercy forgives us and cleanses us from all unrighteousness."

Elizabeth had watched the entire sermon mesmerized by the love that was coming from his eyes as he gave the most stirring message she had ever heard. Her hometown Jackson was smack dab in the middle of the Bible belt, and they were faithful worshipers at West Jackson Baptist Church. She had even made that walk down the aisle when she was twelve and became baptized in water the very next Sunday. That seemed so long ago. *How have I strayed so far from being that girl?*

"There is no sin that cannot be forgiven, except the unpardonable sin of turning your back on the Holy Spirit. As long as you walk by faith, like Moses, as long as you remain pliable in the Master's hands, and repentant, there is hope for you, my friend." He paused for effect. "Do not turn away from the Spirit's call, for we are not guaranteed tomorrow." She knew there was truth in what this man of God was saying. She knew that she had done wrong. This was the consequence of her sin. She wanted forgiveness. She wanted mercy. She wanted to go back to when she was twelve and unmarred by life and naive about worldly temptation. But there was no going back. She had wrapped her arms around her belly and squeezed, weeping and convulsing in wrenching waves. She could not kill this innocent life inside her. *I can't go through with it. There's got to be a way out.* She would ride the bus back to Jackson. She would find Crystal, and they would make a plan. She would tell her parents. *But will they ever forgive me? Can they?*

Beth had lain for what seemed like hours pondering the question, and finally, around 4 a.m., she had succumbed to her exhaustion and slept, tossing with dreadful dreams. In front of her loomed the mummy of a long dead Pharaoh. He was moaning for her to turn back. Turn back. But even as she turned, she faced the horrible jaws of an angry alligator, waiting to devour her whole as she slipped and slid and fell, scrambling to find her parents in the dense fog hovering over the treacherous banks of a very muddy Nile.

Chapter 3
Missing

"And they were grieved because of the Children of Israel..." Exodus 1:12

John Merriweather sat at his breakfast table in black sweat pants, t-shirt, and well-worn slippers, drinking his first cup of Folgers and reading the headlines from *The Jackson Sun,* as was his usual Saturday morning habit. He worked over sixty hours a week as the CFO of a large manufacturing plant on the east side, and so on Saturdays he liked to wind down. A plate of half-eaten pancakes and sausage links rested before him growing colder by the minute, while at his feet, his beloved Setter, Angel begged for a bite of the syrupy remains. Carolyn Merriweather stood at the sink, rinsing her plate and remarking what a mild day it was for January. She was tall and graceful, and her blonde hair was beautifully coiffed from the morning's trip to the salon. The crocus would appear before long if it kept this up, she remarked. John was too engrossed in the feature story to answer her.

"Are you even listening to me, John?"

"Uh-huh, heard every word."

"What did I say then?"

"You said, 'The crocus are going to come up too soon this year.'"

"Okay. So you were listening. Anything good in the paper this morning?"

"The King Tut exhibit got robbed last night in Memphis. They got away with several pieces. I can't imagine who would want them. Wouldn't it be hard to sell artifacts?"

"Maybe they want them for themselves."

"Or maybe the thieves were paid a pretty penny to obtain them for someone's collection. You can bet they won't surface any time soon. Unless the cops get a break on the case pretty quick. Would you get me some more coffee?"

"Does it say how they did it?"

"Actually, it's quite the mystery. There were guards on duty all night. No one saw or heard anything. The curator of the exhibit found the display case empty this morning and reported the theft."

"May be an inside job then," Carolyn answered as she set

27

his steaming cup before him.

"Someone must have wanted them awful bad."

"What were they worth?"

"I'm guessing no one really knows. Quite priceless I'm sure--five solid gold rings with royal insignias embossed on them inside a small treasure chest and a five-pound golden idol." John remarked as he passed Angel a sausage link.

"Says here that one of the rings was actually found on King Tut's mummy, on the middle finger of his left hand. 'The bezel is engraved with a figure of the king kneeling and holding in his outstretched hands an image of the goddess Maat, who is seated overshadowed by a protecting falcon,'" he read. "And then it goes on to describe the other items."

"That's interesting. Maybe we should go see that exhibit, that is, if they keep it open after this."

"Yeah, we'll plan that up. What do you have on your mind for today? The house is so quiet without Beth here."

"Just gonna putter around the house a bit. Thought we might take in a movie tonight at the new theater if she's not too tired from her slumber party."

"Bet she will go straight to bed. But I wouldn't mind seeing "Rumor Has It."

"Chick flick."

The doorbell interrupted Carolyn before she could defend her choice. They looked at each other in surprise. It was only 9:30 a.m., and Saturdays in the Merriweather household were generally subdued. Carolyn did her grocery shopping in the afternoons or browsed the bookstores and Bed Bath and Beyond for bargains. John liked to check out the power tools at Home Depot or prowl around at Buck & Bass. Most often, he liked to stay at home and play with his woodworking tools in the garage. Beth would sleep until noon, then go out with her friends, or get her nails done at the mall. Rarely did they entertain even the neighbors before 11 a.m. on Saturdays, unless John was going hunting.

"You get it honey. I need to finish here."

John laughed. "Yes, but your hair sure is pretty, don't you want to show it off?" he teased. "It's probably just the paper boy collecting."

John was only a bit surprised to find that it was Chris. He was dressed in jeans, a white t-shirt, and his football jacket.

29

"I'm sorry, Mr. John, did I wake you?"

"Oh no, not at all. We're just a bit lazy on Saturdays, Chris. Beth's not here. She spent the night at Crystal's."

"Oh. Well, okay. She didn't call me last night when she got off work. "

"Maybe she just needed a girls' night. She'll be home this afternoon sometime, I'm sure."

"Thanks, Mr. John."

"Uh-huh. See ya later."

Chris dialed his cell phone before he ever reached his car. He thought Beth might want to spend the day with him, but after several tries, it was obvious she was avoiding him for some reason. It irritated him that she had not called last night. He would have understood. He got the voice mail. Her phone was turned off. He left a message for her to call him and then dialed another number. The phone rang twice before Crystal's mother answered.

"Hi, Mrs. Barnes. This is Chris Daily, Beth's boyfriend. May I speak to her a moment, please."

"Oh hello, Chris. Beth's not here. Is she supposed to be?"

"I guess I misunderstood. Is Crystal home?"

30

"Sure. Hold on. I'll get her."

Where in the world was she? This did not make any sense.

"Hello."

"Crystal. This is Chris. Do you know where Beth is?"

"Um...no...um... I thought she was with you."

"I haven't seen her since school yesterday."

Crystal's mind raced. "Well, if she's not with you, then where is she?"

"Her father said she spent the night with you."

"She just told them that because she was spending the night with you, though. That's what she told me."

"What? Why would she do that?"

"I don't know. She said she wanted to be with you. What do we do now? I don't want to get her in trouble."

Look, Crystal. She wasn't with me. She wasn't with you. Something's wrong. Someone has to find out where she is."

"Stay there. I'm coming over. We'll talk to them together. That way, Beth can blame both of us."

Good idea."

Ten minutes later Crystal pulled up in front of the

31

Merriweather's home. He fidgeted a bit, shifting his weight from foot to foot before reaching to ringing the bell. John was puzzled when he opened the door to find both Crystal and Chris at the door.

"Um…may we come in for a moment?"

"Okay." John said slowly. "Where's Beth?"

Chris took the lead. "We don't know, Mr. John."

"She didn't spend the night with me like she told you," began Crystal.

"What?"

"She told me she was going to Chris's and to cover for her." Crystal looked down at the floor, her face flushed with dread and embarrassment.

"What!" He yelled for Carolyn; his eyes widened, his face flushed in anger. "She told you what?"

"She said she was going to spend the night at Chris's and not to tell you if you called. Then, they were going to spend the day shopping."

"Well, where is she then, Chris?" Chris shook his head in helpless angst.

32

"I have no idea; I haven't seen her since school yesterday. Honest. She didn't call me from Wal-Mart either last night."

"What's going on, John. Why are you yelling?" Carolyn asked as she entered.

"Beth didn't spend the night at Crystal's. She told Crystal she was spending the night with Chris. Chris says he hasn't seen her since school yesterday."

"Spend the night? With Chris?"

"How long have you been sleeping with our daughter?" John demanded, taking Chris by the collar. "Since when does she lie to her mom and me—never-- until she started dating you. She never even stayed out past curfew until she met you. She's an Honor student. She wouldn't lay out all night and worry us. What have you done to our daughter?"

"Please Mr. Merriweather. Please don't do this. We have to find her."

"John, please," Carolyn said, "This is not helping find her. Right now we have to find her. Crystal, start calling her other friends. John, call Wal-Mart. Find out what time she left last night-- or if she even went in." Someone had to take charge. Carolyn tried

33

to appear collected and calm.

"I'll call Dana and Samantha, and mom. Maybe she showed up at the house this morning," Crystal said.

Suddenly the horror of what could have happened dawned on Carolyn. Suddenly visions of her daughter lying dead in a ravine in a tangled mass of wreckage crossed her mind. Visions of her bleeding and calling out for help flashed before her. "Something bad has happened, John. I'm calling the police." Carolyn's voice trembled.

'My child has never lied to us. She has never gone somewhere without telling us. She's a good kid. Something's...Hello? Yes, this is Carolyn Merriweather, at 416 Harmony Drive. Our daughter did not come home last night...what? She's seventeen...yes...no...I don't know..." There was a long pause as Carolyn listened to the dispatcher on the other end of the line.

Then, "Please hurry. This is just not like her. She's not a runaway. Please, come quickly. We have to find her." She stood staring at the phone in her hand for a few seconds, as if it were going to ring on cue and it be Beth calling.

"John, where could she be?" And then she began to tremble as if she were standing bare armed at the North Pole. John took her in his arms, took the phone from her, and held her.

"I don't know honey, but we'll find her. She'll be home any minute. Then you can ground her for life--right after I do."

Carolyn pulled back from him. There were tears streaking her face.

"I'm going to check her room. Maybe there's a note or clothes missing. Something..." Carolyn's voice trailed off as she headed upstairs trying to quell the thought that every mother's nightmare had just become her reality.

Beth's room looked like every other seventeen-year-old girl's room, decorated with American Idol posters, concert souvenirs, football items including a warrior headdress with blue feathers, and stuffed animals, mainly teddy bears of all sizes and colors. Her closet door stood open. Clothes were hanging askew from the racks. Shoes were piled in a wild pile in the floor. Makeup was spread out on her vanity; none of it appeared missing, but then Beth had so much that it was hard to tell. Carolyn got on her knees and looked under the bed. Beth's luggage was still there, including her overnight bag. She would have packed that to go to Crystal's. Maybe she hadn't intended to be gone all night. But she had told Crystal she was spending the night with Chris.

Overall, her room looked exactly as it had on any normal day. It was clear that she intended to be home before she was ever missed. Maybe she and another girlfriend had decided to go somewhere. Some concert or something. Something forbidden. But she would have said something. She would have told me. Left me a note, something. Carolyn would never agree to two teenage girls going anywhere overnight without a chaperone, and Beth knew that. That stinker! But where would she have gone? And why would she have used Chris for an excuse with Crystal? Crystal was her best friend. Why wouldn't she have told Crystal what she was really up to?

Carolyn thought back over the last few weeks. Other than Beth missing curfew a couple of times during the holiday break, there was nothing out of the ordinary about her behavior. She had gotten a good scolding from her father the first time it happened. The second time it happened, she was an hour late, and Carolyn and John were both awake. Beth had taken her grounding from the next holiday party in stride. Beth was not a rebellious child. Carolyn wondered about a side of Elizabeth that she never saw. Her eyes went to the computer. Surely she wasn't one of those girls that gets caught up in one of those internet chat rooms, chatting to strangers about God knows what. Surely not. Yet, there were reports in the paper more and more frequently about predators stalking teenage girls on the Internet.

Feeling a bit queasy at the thought, Carolyn reached down and booted the computer. She hardly knew where to begin. She was familiar with the Internet. She was proficient in Microsoft Office, but she had no idea about chat rooms or personals or instant messaging. She opened the browser and hit favorites. There appeared to be nothing out of the ordinary teen realm: a few fashion sites, a music download site, and the high school site. She tried to open the instant messenger panel, but it was password protected. Carolyn hit the history button. There were no sites visited since Thursday night. Elizabeth had logged on, viewed the Yahoo weather page and viewed a few blogs. Carolyn opened each site. There was Crystal's blog, which consisted mainly of cartoons she had drawn and captions. *Nothing unusual there.* There was

37

Dana's blog, which went into every detail of her week from the moment she got up in the morning to the time she went to bed. The only mention of Beth was when Dana mentioned that they worked up a new cheer at cheer leading practice on that day. And finally, there was Beth's personal blog.

Carolyn felt a bit of shame in reading her daughter's personal journal, but it was on the Internet for the entire world to view, she reasoned. *I'll just take a quick peek. She shouldn't have pulled this stunt.* She scanned the short entries for the week:

Monday, January 17, 2005: Out of school for Martin Luther King Day. Slept all day. What a weekend. Posted at 7:00 p.m.

Tuesday, January 18, 2005: Passed the Chemistry exam, whew. I was sweating bullets over that one. Got to keep that grade point up if I'm going to get into Union. Mr.Bradley makes it so unbearably boring. I about fell asleep in class. I guess it's because I stayed out so late over the weekend with Chris. Thought I got caught up on sleep yesterday. I can't stand to be away from him. I think he loves me too. Posted at 4:00 p.m.

Wednesday, January 19, 2005: Just thought I'd post a little note while I had a few minutes before school. I don't really feel like

38

going today. Must have been something I ate. Do hangovers hang over this long? Posted at 7:08 a.m.

That was the last entry for this week. Carolyn cringed at the mention of "hangovers," then backed up to the entries the week before. There were only three entries for the week; only one interested her. It was Sunday's post.

Sunday, January 16, 2005: We had so much fun last night. Chris snuck some bourbon from his dad's liquor cabinet and we drank it and did it in my room. My parents would just kill me if they knew. They don't know what it's like to be young and in love. I just want to have fun before we go off to college in the fall. Don't they know that? Posted at 11:55 p.m.

Carolyn's head reeled from reading the post. Her daughter had been drinking and having sex right there in her own home, right under their noses. How could they have been so blind? If she was doing this and they had no clue, what else was she keeping from them? Were there other boys? Was she drinking all the time? Was she doing drugs too?

Carolyn thought back to that precious August night in 1988 when Elizabeth was born. It had been a grueling labor, but

Elizabeth worth every pain:

"Push! Two, three, four... that's it ...you can do it...seven, eight, nine, and ten. Relax."

Ten long seconds passed as Carolyn struggled through the massive contraction that had rocked her body. No sooner had it passed than she began to feel the next awful wave.

"He's not budging," she grunted through gritted teeth. "Oh, oh...oh…, it's coming! The baby's coming!"

John had been in the birthing room by choice to support his wife during the birth of their first child, and admitted to her later that he almost found himself wishing he were somewhere else. He had no idea that the labor would turn out to be this twelve-hour marathon. His arms ached, he said, from helping to hold Carolyn's legs as she pushed. Yet he still was so handsome in his rumpled shirt with his eyes bloodshot, and the usual five o'clock shadow sprouting. How she loved that man.

John had seen her through ten long, desperate years of trying to conceive. She blamed herself. At sixteen, she had made some unwise choices and gotten into trouble. And although the pregnancy ended in the first trimester with a miscarriage, it had taken years for Carolyn's parents to forgive her. *If I hadn't moved out into my own apartment, I never would have met him*, she thought. She remembered the Italian restaurant where she landed her first job as a waitress. *What was the name of that restaurant? Baudo's. That's it.* It was there she had met him -- a grad student working on his MBA. She was 21; he was 23. It was love at first sight.

She smiled as she remembered the night a few months later when John proposed over dinner. Crying, Carolyn weakly poured out her past to him, but John just sat there and held her hand. In spite of her past, her faults, her flaws -- in spite of everything, he had chosen to love her. She was his. Together they had built a beautiful three-bedroom home on the north side of town while she got her degree, and John worked his way up the corporate ladder.

The pastor. Someone should call the pastor, Carolyn thought. After they got married, they had joined John's home church and begun attending regularly. It was at this church, West Jackson Baptist that Carolyn had gotten saved. It was under the pastor's gentle counsel that she learned to forgive, for although she was back in the good graces of her parents after marrying John, she was still bitter about their response to her in time of trouble. And she

41

was having an even greater problem forgiving herself for the child she had lost.

Nightmares about the baby would plague her. Was it a boy or a girl? Would it have favored her? Could he have become president some day? It took many counseling sessions with John and their pastor to convince her that she had been held in bondage by her past. She had been forgiven by her parents, by John, and by God. She must now forgive herself. Oh how she remembered those nights when John would hold her as she cried and begged God for a child.

But what a celebration they had had when she found out she was finally going to be a mother. *Thank you, God, that you answered my prayer. Thank you for giving me another chance.*

She could still hear John soothing her in the delivery room, encouraging her.

"Just a little longer, honey. You can do it."

"I'm so tired -- so tired."

"Two, three, four," the doctor began.

"Oh...ohh..."

"Seven, eight, nine, and ten. Good job, Carolyn. The head

is out!" And then everything grew quiet.

"What is it?" John asked. The concern was etched in his forehead.

The doctor was strangely silent. Instead another contraction hit, and Carolyn could not hold back. She pushed the baby out, and then fell heavily back to bed.

"Is it a boy?" she remembered asking.

"It's a girl," the doctor answered quietly, still not revealing the cause for his concern. John was so horrified when he left the head of the bed. His little girl was blue. The umbilical cord had been wrapped around her neck, and the doctor was deftly working to revive the infant.

"Why isn't she crying? What's wrong with her? Oh God, someone please say something."

Finally after doing infant CPR, the doctor noted a pulse. He held the baby up by its ankles and smacked her bottom --a practice he had long abandoned. The baby coughed hard and inhaled sharply. A loud wail erupted in the birthing room, and everyone else exhaled a collective sigh of relief. *I was so scared for my little Beth.*

43

Satisfied that the infant was going to be okay, the doctor wrapped her in a warm towel and placed her on Carolyn's belly.

"Ready to meet your daughter, Mrs. Merriweather?"

"She's so beautiful."

John was wiping tears of joy from his eyes and managed to find his voice.

"You sure make beautiful babies, Mrs. M."

"You're not too shabby yourself, big guy," she had said.

So long ago, and yet it seemed like yesterday. Carolyn had had seventeen years of joy, seventeen years of smiles and infectious giggles to warm her heart. But now Beth was missing. And there was this blog that opened the door to a world of fears that was new for Carolyn. Her chin dropped to her chest with a pitiful groan and her body erupting in deep sobs just as John entered the room.

"Honey," he began softly and placed a hand on her shoulder, "the police are here now.

45

Chapter 4
Led into Captivity
"And there rose up a new king in Egypt.' Exodus 1:8

Checkout time was approaching. Beth showered and changed clothes and brushed her teeth, then promptly gagged and dry heaved. The first order of business would be to get something into her stomach. Then she could walk to the bus stop. The continental breakfast in the lobby had already shut down, so she settled for the Waffle House next door. She left the room keys on the television set and pulled the door to behind her.

She walked to the lobby and out the doors unnoticed; the clerk was too busy with paperwork from the night before to even look up. Beth crossed the parking lot and walked over to the Waffle House. There were several cars in the parking lot. She recognized the two-tone GMC from the day before. *Maybe he stopped by here to sober up before his trip home.* She wondered if he had hit it big at the tracks like he thought he would. She could not imagine what fun lay in throwing away everything on such a risky enterprise. But then wasn't that exactly what she had done? Rolled the dice and lost. Big time. Beth swallowed the hard lump in her throat and entered the building.

As soon as she smelled the fresh coffee and greasy bacon frying, she began to feel the nausea welling up in her throat. It was beginning to irritate her. She wondered how many months she would have to endure it. She wondered about a lot of things. Would her parents let her raise the baby? Was adoption an option? Could she give her baby away to strangers?

Chris would have to be told; her father would insist on it. She didn't want Chris marrying her out of obligation. She wasn't even sure she was ready to be married, but ready or not, she was going to be a mother. Another wave of nausea hit her, and she raced to the ladies' room to dry heave again.

When she came out of the restroom, she was so addled that she ran smack into someone.

"Oh. I'm sorry, sir. I wasn't looking."

"No problem, little missy," the dirty white man grinned. "Sure is a fine day ain't it?"

"Yeah it is," she replied and hurried to a table that was sandwiched between two families. A tall and bony waitress with black circles under her eyes and a pencil stuck behind her ear made her way to the table and took her order.

Chocolate milk sounded good to Beth, and grilled cheese, and maybe she would try some oatmeal as well. She was not sure how any of it would set on her stomach, but she was ravenous by this time.

Catfish Bones, a.k.a, Phineas Jones, exited the men's room and made his way to a bar stool at the counter. He kept turning his head her way, as if wondering if she recognized him from the day before. After he was seated, he looked over his shoulder again. It was her. He was certain. *Wonder what that lil filly is doing here? Someone just passin' through should be long gone by now. Did she suspect something? Was she one of those undercover agents he had heard about? They trained 'em mighty young these days. No one would imagine that little slip of a girl to be a DEA officer. That would make the perfect cover. I better watch myself.*

"Give me a coffee, black, hash browns smothered and covered, and three scrambled eggs with toast."

"You got it, sir. Comin' right up," the skinny waitress replied.

He turned on his bar stool to face Elizabeth and seeing she was within earshot, he fished a bit.

"You, little lady, you from around here?" Elizabeth looked up, surprised that he had spoken. She looked around. The place was full of customers. No harm in answering him. He was just making small talk.

"Not too far from here. I stayed at the Horseshoe a little too long last night. Missed the casino ride back."

"Oh is that so? You have any luck over there?"

"Nope. Not a bit. Just kept trying to win my money back," she lied. "How about you?"

"I, uh, come to town occasionally to do a bit of gambling on the dogs," he lied right back.

"You have any luck last night?" she asked.

"I didn't do too bad for an old geezer. Was out rather late myself. Just headed back home. Thought I'd grab a bite first."

"Didn't I see you over there at the Shell yesterday?" Elizabeth asked, but soon regretted it. By the look on his face, he

49

remembered her too, and was not pleased.

"Uh...yep...me and Carnel is track buddies. He didn't hit a lick all night. Was all broke up about it too."

"Sounds like he has my kind of luck."

Elizabeth played with the oatmeal, stirring it in small circles. They had brought the man's food by now, and he had turned back to his plate and was putting the food away. *If he comes to Memphis to gamble with that Carnel, then why did he have to follow him to the track? And what was he doing putting horse feed in the back of Carnel's car?* She remembered seeing a couple of horse farms advertised along the way to Memphis. "Tennessee Walking Horses For Sale, Pine Hill Stables," one sign had read near the Brownsville exit. Maybe Carnel did raise horses.

Elizabeth choked down as much of the breakfast as she could stand. She placed a tip on the table and headed for the register, taking her chocolate milk with her. She asked for a to-go cup as the waitress rang up her check.

"I'm a headed your way if you need a ride, missy. Don't mind a little company."

"That's okay. I'm going to catch a bus back."

"Well, yore welcome to ride with me, if you ain't skeered of a good ol' boy like me."

"Thanks just the same, but I'm not quite ready to leave town." Elizabeth paid the ticket and headed back to the restrooms. The man's body odor had sent her morning sickness into overdrive.

Catfish paid his tab and headed out to the truck to do a bit of thinking. He put a dollar into the newspaper machine and drew out a paper. The robbery had made front page. He quickly scanned the article. No suspects, no leads. "Police frantic to find leads and suspects before the trail goes cold," he mumbled. *She saw me with Frankie last night. If Frankie's body is found, there will be an investigation. The girl can put me in Memphis at the time of the robbery. She's a loose end. Even if she's not DEA, she's seen me.* He would wait for her to come out from the Waffle House. He would just have to make sure she never made it the bus station. There were plenty of places back home to hide a body. He had not come this far and gotten in this deep to spend the rest of his life in the penitentiary. Such a shame. She was such a pretty young thing too. Maybe he would carry her up in the hills a few days and have some fun with her first.

Catfish cranked the old truck and started the heater. It was

51

another mild day in the 50's, but his blood and bones were ice cold. He was too old to make these runs. He was going to retire and build a brick and mortar home with indoor plumbing soon. Soon, if everything went well. Everything must go as planned; the future depended upon it. He had too much at stake to turn back now.

"An Amber alert has just been issued for the states of Tennessee, Kentucky, Arkansas, Alabama, Mississippi, and Georgia. The missing child is 17-year-old Elizabeth Morgan Merriweather, from Jackson, Tennessee, last seen on her job at Wal-Mart on Vann Drive yesterday evening around 7 p.m. She is 5'5, blonde-haired, blue eyed, and was believed to be wearing blue jeans, a blue top, and white Nike tennis shoes. Police believe she may be a runaway as no sign of foul play has been found at this time."

So she was a runaway. She didn't run far. Spent the night in Memphis. Not too smart a cookie is she. This should be easy enough. But the cops are looking for her. It does draw some attention away from the robbery, though. Two hours from now, we'll be in the clear. They will never find her.

Elizabeth had not come out of Waffle House. He was parked right in front of the building. She had not even returned from the restrooms. He would act quickly, corner her in the little hallway, and have a little discussion about her predicament. She would go with him, he was sure of it. He would promise her safe harbor. He would promise her whatever she wanted. But she would go with him.

Catfish left the engine running and went inside. He made his way back to the restrooms unnoticed by the busy waitress. Beth was exiting when he grabbed her arm, pushed her against a wall, and blocked her passage. The restrooms were around a corner. No one could see. He would just have to back off if someone rounded the corner. Beth gasped in surprise, then fear overtook her.

"What do you want?"

"You're that runaway from Jackson aren't you? I just heard it on my radio," he spoke in low tones.

"What? How..."

"They are looking for you. Weren't too smart to stay this close to home last night. They'll find you for sure."

"But...how...I mean...no one knows I'm gone."

"They do now. And everyone's looking for you. You're in a heap o' trouble, missy. What you gone and done?"

"Nothing...I... they're going to kill me." Beth was

53

hyperventilating now what he was said sank in. "My parents must be worried sick. I have to get home."

"If you go to the bus station, they will recognize you. They will call the police. Even if you're going home, you're going to cause everyone a lot of trouble. The police won't be happy with you for wasting their time. Why don't you let me drop you off in Jackson? I'll drop you at the mall. You can then explain to your parents without having to have the police haul you in, in front of all the news and camera crews."

"You're right. My parents will just die. I am so stupid." She was crying now, grieving at what she knew the plan had cost her. She had taken a fast track to hell, and it just kept getting worse.

"Now straighten your face up, Missy. I'll get you home where you belong. Just walk out like me and you's is buddies. No one will know the wiser, especially since you've changed outfits."

Elizabeth dried the tears on the sleeve of her navy sweat suit. She wished she had a hat, or some sort of jacket with a hood. But the weather was too warm, so she had left her coat in the car, along with her Wal-Mart vest and her purse. She took only her wallet and cell phone and had put both of them in the backpack she now carried, which she was thinking now, was way too conspicuous. Together they walked out casually and got in the truck, which was still idling,

Beth had to slam the door of the truck twice to get it to stay shut. The floorboard was littered with beer cans and trash, the ashtray loaded with old butts, the seats were ripped and torn. She looked out the dirty windows and sighed.

"What will we do if we get stopped between here and home?" she asked.

"Well, I sorta doubt they will be looking for traffic coming into Jackson. They probably will be checking the traffic leaving town. If you kinda get down in the floor there, we're not likely to be stopped." Catfish answered.

He, too, had wondered what the plan was. If he could just make it the Law Road exit outside of Jackson, he could hit Highway 412 to Lexington, go through Parsons, and be well on his way to Perry County in no time. The most dangerous leg of the journey would be on the Interstate from the Jackson city limits to the outer limits, about a twelve-mile stretch.

"You get down in the floorboard there. Put all that junk up

55

in the seat. We only have to go about an hour. If we get stopped, we just get stopped." He looked over his shoulder. "Keep your fingers crossed Missy. Catch you a nap. It'll all be all right. Old Catfish gonna see to it."

Beth began pulling all the trash up onto the seat beside her, piling it on top of the *Commercial Appeal* that Catfish had been reading. She made her way to the floorboard and laid her head over on the seat. Catfish almost felt sorry for the girl; she looked so scared. He took his old camouflage jacket from off the back of the seat and covered her with it, making sure her head was covered so that no passing traffic could see her. He would stay in the outside lane making it harder for the big semis to look down inside. Then he put the pedal down and tried not to speed as headed east making his way back toward home.

The truck pulling to a stop awakened Beth. Startled, she poked her head out from under the jacket.

"What is it? Is it a State Trooper? Are we there yet?" Catfish was reaching for her backpack. He did not answer her. She kept asking.

"What is it?"

56

She scrambled up to her seat. They were sitting in a narrow gravel drive, a boat slip at the water's edge. The Tennessee River was spread out before her. There were no boats or barges in sight, just a few ducks flying overhead as foaming white caps made their way ashore. Her eyes widened in fear.

"Where are we? This isn't Jackson. You've passed Jackson. Where are you taking me?"

"Hush, child," he hissed. I had to bring you. I passed too many cops on the way down. No good place to drop you off. Besides, you was running away anyhow. What have you got to go back to? I got a cabin in the hills. You can live with me. Keep me company. No one has to know where ya went."

"But I want to go home. What are you doing.?"

Catfish was taking the clothes out of her backpack by now. He emptied the wallet of its remaining cash and stuck it in his pocket. He put the wallet back, along with the cell phone. "What are you doing!"

"I'm ditching your backpack in the river. Now hush before I ditch you there. And don't think I won't do it. You're becoming more of a problem for me than I expected."

"Just let me go. I'll hitch back to town. I won't say anything. I promise. I promise I won't."

" Now, Missy, don't you think they are gonna wonder where you been all this time?"

"I won't tell them I promise. Let me go or I'll scream."

"No use screaming. Ain't no one for miles around. Might as well settle down. I'd hate to have to use this." Catfish pulled a long knife from the crevice of the seat, and Beth almost wet her pants. Sweat was forming on her upper lip. She felt like retching. *He's going to hurt me. He's going to kill me. Oh God. What have I done? Oh Lord, please, please don't let him kill me.*

He went around to the back of the truck and pulled out a heavy brick he kept back there to brace his tires on steep inclines. He put it inside the backpack and gave it a hard fling out into the water and watched it sink. If anyone did find it, he and the girl would be long gone. They would think she was dead--a victim of suicide or foul play. It didn't matter. No one gave much thought to the fate of runaways anymore. They would think she had ended up in an overseas brothel more than likely. He got back into the truck and started it.

58

"Where are you taking me?" Beth asked.

"So far out in the sticks, no one will ever find you. Just 'til the heat is off. Then, if you still want to go home, you can leave. I can't risk being in the public eye. Not right now. I promise, if you behave, I won't hurt ya none."

She slumped against the seat. Her mouth was dry.

"I need something to drink. I'm going to be sick." He passed her a Dr. Pepper that had been lying in the seat, half drunk and hot.

"That'll have to do, I reckon."

Catfish put the truck in gear and hauled it back up the hill to the main road. He took a right at the top of the hill and headed back to the entrance of Mousetail Landing State Park. Then he made a left onto Highway 412, and sighed a breath of relief as he entered his vast wooded kingdom. It was good to be home.

59

Chapter 5

Life in Pharaoh's Kingdom

"And they made their lives bitter with hard bondage."

Back on the main highway, Catfish and Beth passed an old
church on the left, Howard's United Methodist Church. They made
a couple of hair-raising turns away from the river. Beth could see
the charred impressions on the guardrail where someone had met
their fate on the dangerous curve. She held her breath as they
maneuvered the bend, but Catfish seemed oblivious to any danger.
He was on home turf now. All urgency was gone. He even let her
sit up in the seat as long as she ducked down when they met the
occasional car.

Beth noticed there was little traffic on this highway. She

wondered where they were going as she tried to burn the route into her memory. Every edifice, every bridge, every creek's name they passed, she repeated silently to herself. She dared not break the silence after his threats to dispose of her.

Unlike West Tennessee, once they had crossed the Tennessee River, the landscape transformed into rolling hills reminiscent of the Smokies farther east. The road twisted and curved, ascending and descending in its winding path. The trees were all bare allowing her to see straight through them and view hilltop homes. It amazed her that people were able to get their vehicles up such steep inclines. A few homesteads dotted the roadside, simple frame houses or mobile homes with peculiar homemade shelters built over them. Beth wondered if this was to protect the trailer from falling trees and limbs.

They passed another church, The Church of Latter Day Saints on the left, and Beth assumed they were coming into a more populated area, but her hopes were squashed with the passing miles. A few more homes with grazing horses, a few more mobile homes, and a few home businesses popped up, but nothing that appeared to be a city. They passed a sign that indicated a home for troubled

61

teens on the left. She had been to Nashville before, so she assumed that everything between Jackson and Nashville was well populated and thriving. The only thing she could see thriving out the window was wildlife. Yet, there seemed to flow a simple serenity that she assumed most of the people who lived in this area enjoyed. That would be its only plus, she imagined.

After about fifteen miles, they began another steep ascent and at the top of the hill made yet another sharp s-curve. Beth looked down in the vast gully below. It was a long way to the bottom. A sawmill was in operation right on the curve. At last, some form of life presented itself. Once they navigated the curves, what lay in the valley before them was the idyllic little town of Linden. Beth began to see more houses, a few more businesses, a couple more churches. Soon they were at a red light. She could see the court square on her left. A couple of old trucks were parked on the square, but there was not a person in sight.

"You best be ducking down now I suppose. And don't you raise up 'til I tell you to. I don't need no questions about who I'm cartin' around, ya hear?"

"Okay," Beth answered meekly as she got back down to her

hiding place in the floorboard. Could she reach the door handle? She could jump out and escape. What if she hurt the baby? Did she have a chance of surviving if she stayed in the truck? She was wondering what to do when she felt the truck make a right and go down a hill. Mentally she tried to keep track of the turns and hills, so that she could find her way back. They had gone maybe a half a mile in this direction when she felt the truck stop and idle, a stop sign or traffic light, she guessed. Then, the truck roared back into life as it crossed the intersection. Catfish blew his horn in a short greeting as he passed, not seeming to fear the attention. Beth did not realize that not to have blown or waved would have created more attention in this friendly county where everyone was related.

The whole county's population was only about 8,000 people, almost all of them kin. There was a grand total of one grocery store in a town that boasted two banks, one post office, and six churches. This county had one high school, one middle school, and two elementary schools, which was not much civilization for a county that covered four hundred and eleven square miles. She could not know that there wasn't even a Wal-Mart or a McDonald's or that the county had one, fifty-bed hospital and two clinics, for a total of

63

seven doctors and one dentist. Teachers and nurses held the high

paying jobs in this county, along with a few factory workers and

loggers of the major timberlands.

The Buffalo River ran along the eastern edge of the county

and meandered its way through both Linden and Lobelville, the two

major towns in the county. Sometimes it flooded with spring rains

as it swelled from the overflow of all the creeks that fed into it, but

generally in the summer months, it was a quiet, lazy river where

tourists flocked to float canoes along certain tamer parts of its

scenic route past rocky ledges and campsites. The Buffalo River had

a channel depth of about five feet normally, making it ideal for

swimming, wading, and fishing. Some spots along its way were so

shallow that canoers would have to get out and pull their canoes

along the gravel bottom toward deeper water. There were side

pools perfect for swimming where adults and children alike could

dive from rocky ledges into the cool green water below. Picture-

perfect post card views could be had by land and by air. It was no

wonder that Perry County was favored for its wild game and

fishing. Being situated between two rivers, the wildlife and

atmosphere were inviting and the people as down-to-earth and decent as they come--for the most part.

On any given day, a customer could park his boots beneath a booth at The Dinner Bell restaurant down behind the high school and be treated to the finest catfish dinner for miles around, including homemade chocolate pie with mounds of meringue. The locals would gather there daily to catch up on the gossip and catch a cup of coffee or unwind after their day. Most Saturdays, old Poke would be seated at a far table, chewing a wad of tobacco and reading old news from *The Buffalo River Review,* the weekly newspaper, while drinking his coffee and waiting for his Poker buddies to join him. They would sit around and jaw about that week's news or sporting events. Basketball was the favored sport. The Perry County Vikings had for years been top contenders in the region. They had finally gotten a football team to boot, as well as a new high school. Of these accomplishments they were most proud.

Today Poke and his buddies would just have to wonder what Catfish Bones was up to when he hadn't shown up for dinner, which is what people around these parts called lunch. They might wonder if he was sick, or think maybe it was Inetha, who rarely ventured into town due to her lupus. The men had a standing

65

Poker night on Thursday nights, and Catfish had left the table a winner this week; so it was also possible Catfish had made a casino run with his winnings. He always came back loaded. Bones had the best luck of anyone Poke knew.

He also knew that Catfish ran shipments of Mary Jane down Memphis way every now and then for extra cash. He hoped that Catfish had not gotten caught. It was unlikely, being as lucky as old Cat was. Still, Poke had to wonder.

He was just about out of his private stash himself. Maybe tonight he would crank up the boat and head down river to Catfish's place and just see what was going on and replenish his stock. Usually Catfish would hear him coming down the river and meet him riverside out of sight of the house, so Inetha would not find out that he was selling pot. He was fairly certain she had no idea about the crop Catfish was growing on the backside of his property, or she would not have stood for it. Inetha was of the opinion that just because a person was poor, it did not make him white trash or dirty. How she and Catfish, or Phineas, as was his given name, fell in love he would never know.

Catfish had told him that he met Inetha at a church box

66

supper. He had bid on Inetha's box because the whole town knew she made the best fried pies in Perry County. That was back when both of them were younger, back before Inetha's health gave out, and Phineas quit attending church--back before he became the river rat drug runner that he was now. Poke remembered a time when Phineas Jones was a decent and honest farmer. But he guessed the claws of poverty had sunk in too deep. The lack of necessities and medical care and a solid roof that did not leak had turned Catfish cynical. He knew Cat had wanted a family and a real home. Hadn't Cat made the remark that he hadn't counted on Inetha letting him down this way? That was pretty cold, even for Catfish.

But Poke didn't realize that Catfish had other friends outside of Perry County. Catfish had never told him about meeting up with Frankie Carnel at the slots one night, and that Frankie, after learning that Catfish was from the stick, had eventually propositioned him about growing the weed and making a little spending money on the side. What it seemed like at the time was the perfect opportunity to get out from under the bondage of poverty. He could get Inetha the medicine she needed. They could build a real home, drive decent vehicles, and retire comfortably. He

67

would claim he had hit it big at Fitzgerald's, and no one would be the wiser. He had not counted on getting involved in a robbery that would lead to murder and kidnapping a teenage runaway. At this point, Catfish was all-in, and the river card was anybody's guess.

The old truck rattled as it hit a pothole here and there. They had traveled on the gravel side road for maybe ten minutes. Once they had cleared town, Catfish had allowed Beth back into her seat. She had finally summoned the courage to ask where they were headed, but he had ignored her request. She could not wait to get wherever it was; she had needed go the restroom ever since they had stopped at the river. Her head ached, and the nausea was still threatening to turn into vomiting. By this time she did not care where he was taking her; she was just thankful to be alive. She had a notion that if he really intended to kill her, he would have done so back at the river. So maybe she still had a chance to get away. She hoped and prayed that she did. Whatever was awaiting her back home would be a picnic compared to this.

They were traveling a gravel road that paralleled the Buffalo River. Beth could see the water below between the trees and beyond the valley on the driver's side. They were climbing a steep embankment, and Catfish had to put the truck into low gear to make the hill. When they reached the top, the land flattened out somewhat, the trees parted, and before them lay the vast, indomitable kingdom of Phineas Jones.

Directly ahead Beth saw what appeared to be a mobile home, although it was so rough and weathered that it could easily be mistaken for abandoned. It was small, maybe fourteen feet by seventy, and a faded salmon color with faded black shutters. The underpinning had been torn off around most of the foundation, and a few chickens ran out from under while being chased by a mangy-looking, half-breed dog, who upon seeing Catfish's truck pull in, ran to greet him with his tail wagging. The front storm door was missing, and concrete blocks served as steps.

The wealth of the kingdom was on grand display, with old vehicle parts strewn about the yard, along with tires and tools and garbage. A fifty-five gallon blue drum sat beside the front door, and was full of briny water. A crude clothesline hung out beside the trailer and was strung between two trees. Beyond that lay the remains of a garden plot trodden down with the tomato sticks still sticking up from the ground, and rags hanging from the dead vines.

69

The grass was brown and patchy with muddy spots in odd places. Plastic covered the windows, but had been blown loose by the wind on the end and was flapping in the January wind. Set against the backdrop of the gray skies of winter, the scene was bleak and cheerless.

"Well, missy, I reckon we're home. Now ain't no use'n hollerin'. Ain't nobody around for miles this time of year. I'm still good fer my promise of throwin' you in the river yonder if you'ns don't behave."

Beth nodded. "I have to go really bad."

"To yer right, inside the door, and first left. And no funny business."

They made their way up the concrete steps. Beth entered slowly, not sure of what she might encounter. The stench hit her nostrils before she had gone two steps inside--the smell of animal waste, human waste, and stale smoke. Spoiled food and rotten garbage lay rotting in plastic bags. She felt her stomach lurch as she hurried down the hall. She flipped the switch for the bathroom and heaved into the toilet, which was black and yellowed and unspeakably nasty. When she was finished, she tried to flush, but nothing happened. She lifted the back off the toilet. No water was running. She turned the faucet in the sink; nothing came out.

Beth pulled back the nasty shower curtain and turned the knobs of the tub. Nothing. But there was a five gallon bucket half full of the briny water. She lifted it out of the tub and poured it into the back of the toilet and flushed.

Elizabeth's mind was reeling. How could a human live in these conditions? She felt dirty and grimy, and now she had to drip dry. There wasn't even toilet paper. She longed for a shower and clean clothes, and then she remembered that she was wearing the only clean outfit she had brought with her. Her dirty clothes were in the truck. She cleaned up the best she could and went back to the living room. "I need clean clothes."

"So skeered you wet your pants, eh? Tomorrow you can haul some river water up here to wash your dirty clothes. I'll make a fire and heat some water in the kettle. Then you can scrub 'em and hang 'em on the line to dry. And unless you're fond of doin' the laundry that a way, I suggest you learn to wear 'em a few days. You must of left home in a hurry. And where'd you get all this here cash? You get caught stealin'?"

71

"I'm not a thief. Or a liar and kidnapper," she spat back. "What are you going to do with me, just keep me out here in the wilderness to be some kind of slave?"

"I ain't decided jest yet. You best be watchin' that sharp tongue. Old Catfish might jest cut it out with this here knife." He took the stainless steel knife off the bar, unfolded it, and pointed it toward her. "This here will skin a buck quicker than you can say 'Jack Rabbit.'"

Beth's eyes widened. She bit her lip, and then the tears began to form and roll down her cheeks. The shock of the last two days began to spill over and out from her, and her shoulders shook in heaving sobs.

"Oh God... God," she cried hysterically. Then she began coughing violent, heaving coughs, as if she were going to throw up again. She could not get her breath.

A look of shock crossed Catfish's face, unnoticed by Beth. He laid the knife on the counter and crossed to where she was. He started to hug her, and then backed off, not knowing exactly what to do with his hands. He put one hand on her shoulder.

"Listen here, missy. Stop crying. Settle down. No use makin' yerself sick again. You act real good. Just settle down. Once they stop lookin' for you and the heat is off, then maybe you can go wherever it is you was a headed. Okay?"

"Okay." Beth mumbled. Catfish took a dirty handkerchief from his back jean pocket and held it out to her. She took it, hesitated slightly, then dried her face. "Can I please just have a drink?"

"What you want, a beer? Naw, of course not. I got a Coke. I got a little bit of drinking water left...hafta get more tomorrow down at the store. That dern well man couldn't get through the limestone. Wanted six thousand dollars to haul his fancy equipment all the way out here. I figgered when I got me the money to build the new house, I'd take care of getting' a well dug then. No sense in runnin' a line to this heap of metal."

Her crying had tapered to light sniffling at this point as she sipped from the can of off-brand cola he had handed her. Beth looked around her in disgust.

"Sit down. Youn's been through a lot."

"Why did you take me?" she asked, trying to sound calm as she moved piles old newspaper out of a dumpy green stained recliner.

73

"Well, see, here's the thing," Catfish began. "They had this here Amber alert out on the radio. That's how I figured out who you was. And about two miles before we got into Jackson, right along where I planned to let you out, there was a bunch of State troopers on the other side of the Interstate checking trucks and cars. I had no choice but to roll on through, and the same was happening when I got to the other side of town. Luckily, it was right past the exit I turned off on. I could see the roadblock up ahead of the Law Road exit. By that time, I had done decided that you was on the run for something bad. I just figured it would be easier for you to hide if I brought you up here. You *was* runnin' and hidin, warn't you?"

She did not want to tell him the truth. If he found out she was pregnant, he might go berserk and kill her. So she lied.

"I...uh...was running away to see my boyfriend. He got sent to Memphis to a private military prep school. My parents hated him. I was going to come home after a few days."

"Uh-huh. Sneakin' off to see that there young buck done caused you a heap o' trouble, missy."

If you only knew, she thought, but nodded.

"Yore name's Eliza Beth ain't it?"

"Elizabeth," she answered. "It's Elizabeth."

"That's what I said." And then he said, "Liza," turning it over in his mind as he rubbed the knife up and down against his thigh. "I like that. I reckon that'll do, Liza."

"I bet my mom and dad are out of their minds with worry right now..."

"Didn't think of that did ya? All you was studyin' was getting' with that young buck."

"No, at the time, I just wanted out."

"Well I reckon we all feel that a way at times. Been there myself. Just take a look around at my world. You probably had it real good back there in Jackson, now didn't ya?"

"Yeah, I guess I did. Can I have something to eat?"

"Pickled baloney and Saltines. Take it or leave it. Get up and fix us a bite. You might as well earn yer keep. Crackers is on the table. Baloney in the fridge." Beth just stared at him. *Is this coot for real?*

Catfish settled into the dirty recliner and flipped on the television. It was a bit early for news, so he settled on reruns while

75

Beth fixed their supper. The day was fading fast into night; sundown came early in the winter months. They ate in silence and watched reruns until the five o'clock newscast out of Nashville came on the air. Catfish turned up the volume as the newscaster recounted the story of the search for the missing teen.

"The search for 17-year-old, Elizabeth Morgan Merriweather, has turned up empty handed as investigators search for clues in a desperate bid to find her in the critical hours of the investigation. Her abandoned car was found in the parking lot of Wal-Mart where she worked part time after school. They found her purse, minus her wallet and cell phone. She is believed to be a runaway, as there is no indication of foul play at the present time. A widespread search is being conducted in the five counties of Madison, Gibson, Crockett, Henderson, and Hardeman. Roadblocks set up along the Interstate earlier today yielded no leads. Carolyn and John Merriweather are here to make a desperate plea for their daughter's safe return." The reporter held the microphone in front of Carolyn. Her face was etched in sorrow. Her voice trembled.

"Beth, if you're watching out there somewhere, please,

76

please call us and let us know you're alright. Your father and I are worried sick about you. We love you, and whatever is bothering you, we can work this out. If anyone knows of our daughter's whereabouts or has taken her, please contact us so that we can meet your demands. We want our daughter back...please...." and her voice trailed off in sobs as John stepped forward.

"Beth, please come home soon to us. We are looking for you. We love you. We want you home with us." The reporter gave a hotline number for anyone with any information to call in and report to the police and then gave a grim sign-off before the broadcast was switched back to the main anchorwoman. Catfish turned off the TV. The two sat in silence for a space of thirty seconds before Beth spoke.

"They're looking for me. They will find me, eventually. And you will face jail time for kidnapping. Is that what you want?"

"I didn't *want* any of this to happen, but I had no choice. You're here now. I can't afford for them to find you. I can't let you go home. You, you just know too much."

"What do you mean?"

"Even if I let you go home, you'll tell them. You can

77

identify me. I'd be running the rest of my life."

"I won't tell. I swear I won't.

"I can't trust you. I have too much at stake. There's too many things goin' on. I can't afford for them to find out about Frankie. They'll kill me."

"Frankie? They who?"

"Carnel. Frankie Carnel. The man you saw me with yesterday. I know you saw. I saw you staring right at us."

"What's he got to do with anything?"

"Frankie has everything to with everything."

Just as Beth thought she was going to hear the rest of the story, a boat motor from down at the river interrupted. Catfish jumped up, knocking over his beer.

"Dang. That's Old Poke. Stay in the trailer and clean that up. Or I will make you wish you never been born."

He ran out the door and down the concrete steps. It had grown dark, and there was no security light. Even though Beth stared out the blinds, she could not see what was happening. She thought about running, but she knew she would not get far in this wilderness. She wondered if Catfish had left the keys in the old

78

truck. Her thoughts wandered back to the knife. If she ran to the truck and there were no keys, could she make it back to the house before Catfish? She had no idea how far away he was. She wondered who Old Poke was. Was that another thug Catfish hung out with? And who was Frankie Carnel? Part of a crime ring? Whoever he was, Catfish was terrified of any retribution at his hands. She had gotten herself tangled in a mysterious web of danger and deceit. She knew she had to get to that truck.

Slowly she turned the doorknob, cracked the door, and listened. She could hear voices, but they were moving farther away. She stepped out onto the first step. Then she ran as fast as she could toward the rusty old truck. She was hassling for breath when she got to the truck door. When she opened the door, it let out a long creak. She felt strong arms grab her from behind and swirl her around.

"Just where do you think you're goin', Liza Beth? Home to Mama?"

"I...uh...I...was coming to get my other clothes."

"Don't you lie to me," Catfish spat out. "You was makin' a run for it." He reached inside, grabbing the keys from the ignition.

79

He grabbed her clothes from the floorboard and flung them at her.

"You just better be glad I stopped you. I know where you're from, Missy. I would track you down and put a bullet in yer purty skull. Now back in the house. Now!"

Elizabeth was breathless in her sobbing pleas.

"Please...please just let me go home. Please, I beg you… Please." She fell to her knees in the wet grass in despair, begging for her life.

Catfish's expression softened. He reached down and took her by the arm and helped her up. He took out the dirty bandana and wiped her face roughly.

"You got to stop this. I can't let you go. I done told you. My life is in danger. Stop crying. Just dry up," he said, trying to appear gruff but his voice had softened. He pulled her to him; she was soft and pretty. It had been a long time since he had held a woman. Thoughts began to form in his deluded mind that she could grow to like him. He could keep her here forever. She would be his. His hands found the bottom band of her sweatshirt and swiftly they found their way underneath. Elizabeth was startled as his hands grabbed at her. She screamed and pushed him away.

"No. No...stop it!" She pulled back, but he held her firmly.

80

"No use fightin' it missy. We're gonna spend a lot of time together up in these hills. Might as well make it fun."

"No, Oh please, no."

He had jerked her back to his chest, and his hands were headed down the back of her sweatpants. He was rubbing his beard against her neck and making noises in his throat like he was enjoying making her squirm. The bile rose up in Beth's throat.

"Oh God, Stop! I'm going to be..." but before she could finish her sentence, the vomit was up and out and all over the two of them, splattering all over Catfish and Beth. He let her go. She was choking and bent double. She could not breathe. Catfish was stunned by this event. He had never had a woman throw up at the thought of being with him. Shame burned bright in his cheeks.

"I weren't gonna hurt ya, missy. I swear. I thought you might like it. Might need some comfortin'."

"I'm seventeen. I'm only in high school," she choked out. "I don't want you. Why would I want you? You're dirty. You stink. You chew tobacco and drink beer. Oh no..." and she bent double and heaved again. By this time she was dry-heaving and hurting.

"I suppose you're right. Been a long time since I cleaned up."

81

His pride was wounded, what little he had. But at least she hadn't

called him stupid.

"I'll get some water heated up to put in the tub. I got a

flannel shirt you can wear. Don't cry. I won't touch you no more.

Just stop crying, for Pete's sake."

Beth took long deep breaths, sighing with relief that he was

not going to rape her, at least not tonight. For the first time this

week, she thanked the Lord for the life that was growing inside her.

Only morning sickness had stopped this ruthless man from taking

her and making her a slave to his fleshly lusts.

Chapter 6
The Search

"And it came to pass..."

Months had passed since Elizabeth's disappearance. The investigation had started with a flurry of activity, then slowed to a crawl. Finally the trail had ended with a reference to Mr. Merriweather's MasterCard being used at the Wingate Inn right outside of Memphis on the day of Beth's disappearance. A girl fitting that description had spent the night at the Wingate, and to the clerk's recollection, she was alone. The clerk could give only the date of checkout and had no knowledge of Beth leaving. She had not worked the weekend shift, the other clerk had; she had not noticed anything out of the ordinary either. This confirmed the police's suspicions that Elizabeth was a runaway. The police questioned Elizabeth's closest friends; they questioned her parents, her relatives, and her teachers. None could give them any reason why Beth would run away from home.

Her textbooks were in her car, as well as her gym clothes thrown in the backseat. There were no notes to indicate why she had left or where she had gone. They rang her cell phone number , to no avail. They tracked her cell phone usage. She had not used the phone since the day she left. There was one call that day to the Wingate Inn at 8:45 p.m. Other than that, there was a call from her boyfriend, Chris at 9:40, Saturday morning with a message for Beth to call him, and numerous messages from Beth's parents begging her to call home. All of those had gone to voice mail. Either Beth had ditched the phone, which was unlikely, or she had it turned off. The police noted that unless she had taken the charger with her, it would soon be of little value to her anyway. The charger was found plugged into the cigarette lighter of her car.

Beth's parents put out a desperate media plea and a hundred thousand dollar reward hoping to get their daughter back. The leads came rolling in faster than the police could follow up on them. Most of them led to dead ends, except for two. One was the bus driver of the casino bus who called to say he remembered a girl matching her description riding the bus to Memphis. He was very sorry to hear that she was a runaway. How could he have known? The other lead matched up with the bus driver's. The Shell clerk had waited on the girl after the bus had departed. She remembered the girl asking for a phone book and buying a map. She said the girl left on foot in the direction of the Wingate. She had paid cash for the map and drink.

The police pieced together that Elizabeth had hopped the casino shuttle bus after her work shift and rode it as far as Germantown. She had gotten off at the Shell on Exit 16, bought a map and a drink, then checked in at the Wingate. After she left there, it was anyone's guess where Elizabeth might have gone. Interviews at the bus stations and cab offices came up empty-handed. Wherever Elizabeth was, she had either walked, hitched, or been forced to go there. She had not used any other form of public transport. Her parents were comforted only in the knowledge that Beth was probably alive and on the run, and most likely still in the Memphis area. The police questioned the employees at the Waffle House, thinking Elizabeth ate breakfast there or at the hotel, but none of the employees could remember.

"Honey, this place stays full on the weekends. Old people, young people, black people, white people...who can keep track of them all. I just try to get my shift done and get home and soak my tired bunions. I can't help you," the waitress glibly answered. The cook was just as helpful.

"Hey, my back's to the crowd all day. I work for a living."

Elizabeth's parents had even made a trip down to Memphis to hand out fliers and put them on cars at the mall. They showed her picture to countless shoppers. They plastered her picture at the bus terminal and the cab stations, and all the public attractions, including the Memphis Zoo. The King Tut exhibit had been closed due to the investigation surrounding the robbery. But they scoured the ballpark, Graceland, and a host of other tourist spots, just in case anyone had seen their daughter. John and Carolyn returned to Jackson distraught and emotionally drained. All they could do now is pray for news.

West Jackson Baptist Church held a candlelit vigil for Elizabeth, and over three hundred students attended. Teachers and friends alike poured into the Merriweather home to comfort and

87

help with the daily tasks. Carolyn had been in a constant state of turmoil. Ladies from the church brought casseroles and made coffee. The men took up an offering from all the Sunday School groups, the choir, the missions groups, every department in the church gave to help pay the Merriweather's expenses while they took time off from work to devote to their daughter's search. A gospel singing was held at The Old Country Store to raise money and awareness for the missing teen. It was a given in the rural South that when your neighbor was in trouble, you were there to help out in any way you could. It was one of the reasons John never considered moving up north. The Hub City was known for making newcomers feel welcomed and loved. He just could not imagine why his daughter would want to leave.

It was mid-April when the officer rang the bell and asked to speak to both John and Carolyn. John trembled as he led the officer in to the living room. The look on the officer's face was not one of joy. It was somber and foreshadowed bad news.

"What is it officer? You've found her." John questioned. Carolyn joined her husband on the sofa and gripped his hand tightly.

"No, we haven't found her. But we have found something. A fisherman snagged Elizabeth's backpack on his fishing line. He drew it out of the Tennessee River near Decaturville. Her wallet and cell phone were inside, along with a heavy brick."

Carolyn gasped. John's eyes narrowed.

"But what does that mean? That's nowhere near Memphis. You mean the Mississippi River?"

"No sir. It was the Tennessee River. We aren't sure at this point what that indicates. I think you must prepare yourself. The backpack being weighted is not a good indication. It could have been used to weight her body." At this comment, Carolyn let out a low, guttural moan of grief.

"No. My baby…no, God, please no."

John held his wife as she sobbed on his shoulder. He patted her back. He ran his fingers through her hair and tried to soothe the ache within her. Yet, his gut was telling him that Beth was gone. Someone had hurt her.

"There's something else I think you should know. Inside the zipper pocket of the backpack was a used pregnancy test. It was positive. We think Elizabeth may have committed suicide by

89

jumping from one of river bridges. There is also the possibility that this is a homicide. We are going to bring in the boyfriend for questioning."

New moans of grief racked the couple's bodies, their horror and disbelief played out in painful detail on their faces.

"Pregnant? Our daughter is *pregnant*? John, how could she not tell us?" Carolyn began.

"That boy got our daughter pregnant. You think he *murdered her?*" John asked incredulously. "He might be a rounder, but…I mean… murder? I'm going to the police station. I'll get the truth out of him if I have to beat it out of him."

"Mr. Merriweather, we prefer you stay here and wait for word from us. We have divers at the site where the backpack was found. If Elizabeth turns up, you will want to be here with your wife. Let us handle the investigation, sir, please."

John swallowed his anger and managed to find his voice, although by this time the vein in his forehead was bulging, and his jaw was tightly clenched.

"Thank you for the information, officer. Please call us as soon as you find her."

Jackson's finest made his farewells and retreated to his police car to radio his whereabouts and where he was headed. John and Carolyn stood in the doorway and cried. Carolyn nuzzled underneath his John's arm like a fragile baby bird awaiting nourishment, awaiting hope, awaiting anything that would bring her daughter and grandchild back alive.

The scene down by the river earlier that morning had drawn a crowd. There was never much excitement in the sleepy little town of Decaturville. Word was out that the river was being searched for a body, a missing runaway. Naturally, folks came to see what they could see. Divers would come up at intervals with odd items such as a pair of sunglasses or an odd flip-flop. Each would be tagged as possible evidence to be shown to the family. Every time a diver would surface the crowd would buzz, wondering if the next item brought up would be the missing girl. The recent media coverage about a pregnant lady missing in California fueled their conversation and thirst for more of the drama that was unfolding before them. This could be a copycat murder. The runaway was pregnant too. A special TBI team with fancy sonographic equipment had arrived to aid the search. Bloodhounds were

91

traversing the banks for any clues.

A reporter from the local weekly paper was on hand interviewing the lead investigator, but there was not much to tell at this point. The investigator relayed what little information they had gleaned from the backpack and gave pertinent information regarding Elizabeth's disappearance back in January. The reporter seemed mildly disappointed, but after having obtained the name of the missing girl and where she was from, hurried back to the office to work up his story. They had been by the riverside most of the day. He doubted that they would find the body today, and he had a deadline to meet. Recovering the body would be next week's story. He was already dreaming of his story hitting the AP wires and making him the star of the next CNN broadcast. He would write the both segments. Just in case.

Chapter 7

A Sad Mother's Day

"She refuses to be comforted for her children"

It had been another difficult day for Carolyn --Mother's

Day. Depressed by the thought of her daughter never returning

home, Carolyn sat cross-legged on her king-sized bed and surveyed

all of the albums before her. She had photographs of Beth

beginning with day one and ending with Christmas 2005. She had

scrapbooks filled with pre-school art and locks of hair. She had

kept every Mother's Day card Beth had ever given her, starting with

her very first, signed by John. It was unfathomable to imagine that this beautiful young girl had come to a tragic end.

Yes, she had spoiled Beth. But she had only wanted to give her a life that Carolyn herself had never known. She wanted her daughter to be popular and well educated, charming, and well groomed. She wanted so much for Beth. Carolyn picked up Beth's first grade snapshot. She had lost her two front teeth, and was extremely self-conscious about it, even at that tender age.

"But mommy, what if they laugh at me?"

"Honey, no one will laugh. All your friends will lose their baby teeth too."

Beth was always worried about what people thought of her. She was such a people pleaser, such a perfectionist. *I did that to her, I suppose*, Carolyn thought. *I wanted her to be perfect. I expected too much from her, pushed her too hard. Why couldn't she come to me? Of all people, I would have understood.* Tears were rolling down her cheeks unchecked.

There was a photograph from a recent vacation. Beth had wanted to go to Dollywood, but John and Carolyn outvoted her in favor of Niagara Falls. Carolyn had snapped the picture of Beth aboard *The Maiden of the Mist*. She stood holding the rail, her rain slicker blowing in the mist, her face sullen and uninterested.

95

Carolyn would give anything to go back in time. Why hadn't they gone to Dollywood like Beth wanted? They could have gone to Niagara after Beth graduated and went to college. Why had they made her come along, when she had insisted she was old enough to stay home alone? *I smothered her -- babied her too much. It's my fault. It's all my fault.*

"Honey...." John began as he entered the bedroom. He stopped short when he saw Carolyn on the bed holding the picture.

"I failed her John. I failed my daughter. She needed me and couldn't come to me when she got in trouble."

"You were ...you *are* a wonderful mother. You can't keep beating yourself up over this. We taught Beth right from wrong. We took her to church. We did everything in our power to protect her. Honey, sometimes bad things happen. We're not better than anyone else. Life's dealt us a sorry hand, babe. But we have to trust that God is in control. I have to trust that God is in control. I have to. That's what gets me through each day."

John tenderly took the photo from her and scooted the album to the middle of the spread. He sat down beside his wife, took her into his arms, and held her. And as he held her, he began to quietly pray for sufficient grace and strength for both of them to

make it through one more day. *Just one more day, Lord.*

Chapter 8
Wrongly Accused
"Why have ye done this thing?"

The investigators working the case knew that the odds of

finding Elizabeth alive after all this time were slim after fishing her

backpack from the Tennessee River and finding out that she was

pregnant. Their attention turned to Chris as the primary suspect.

They began conducting extensive interviews with all of Elizabeth's

school and church friends, asking them about Elizabeth's

relationship with Chris. Most of her girlfriends confirmed that Chris

and Elizabeth were dating. None of them confirmed any sexual

activity between the two, until they interviewed Crystal, who, went

into immediate hysterics when the backpack was found.

"Oh no. She's dead?" Her eyes welled up with tears, her lip

trembled and her hands began to shake as well.

"We don't know that. A body has not been found, despite what the papers released. The reporter was trigger happy. That reporter wrote up the story in anticipation of a body, and mistakenly sent it across the AP wires. All we actually found was the backpack with the pregnancy test inside."

"Pregnancy test?"

"Yes, and since the backpack was waterproof, the test was preserved quite well. It indicated that whoever took the test was pregnant."

Crystal paled. Her eyes widened as she looked away from the investigator's stare.

"Is that news to you, or did you already know?"

"No. I...no...I didn't know." Crystal leaned over the table and buried her head in her hands, sobbing. "I told her to be careful. She swore after the first time they used protection."

"The first time? Who was she sleeping with Crystal?"

"Chris."

"Chris, her boyfriend?"

"Yes."

"Is that the only boy she was sleeping with that you know of?"

99

"Yes."

"She told you she had been with Chris?"

"Yes, after the Homecoming game she came to me and told me they did it in the car out on Bascomb Road."

"She told you this? And the Homecoming game, when was it?"

"Yes. It was back in November. Right before Thanksgiving. You think Chris had something to do with her being missing? Chris wouldn't do anything to her."

"Well, uh, let's just say, we have some questions for him as well. Anything else you can tell us about her relationship with Chris, Crystal?"

"She told me she was spending the night at Chris's the night before she disappeared. I already told you all that. But Chris said he hadn't seen her since school. Chris thought she was at my house. Believe me, he didn't know."

"Well, we will talk to Chris about his whereabouts again. Maybe there are some things Chris hasn't told us."

"Can I go now?"

"Of course, but call us if you think of anything else you can remember. Anything, you understand?"

"Yes sir. Please find her. She's my best friend."

"We hope to find her safe and well. Take care, Crystal."

After Crystal exited, the investigator decided to go to the school and pay a surprise visit to Chris. Interviews went so much better with the suspect if he was caught off guard. He would ask Chris about his sexual relationship with Beth and why he hadn't told the police about it before. He would also get Chris's alibi for the night before. The investigator was sure that Chris had something to do with the young girl's disappearance. He was sure Elizabeth had drowned in the Tennessee River, or been disposed of there.

The biggest piece of the puzzle was why she was in Memphis the night she disappeared. Had Chris taken her to Memphis for an abortion, Elizabeth chickened out, and Chris decided to kill her? The last known trail ended with Elizabeth checking into the Wingate. The keys were left in the room. The clerk did not know what time she checked out. He could have killed her that night, transported her to back through Jackson, then on to the Tennessee River and disposed of her. But that was illogical with

101

the Mississippi River so convenient to the Wingate. But then murderers, especially teenage murderers, were never logical. It did not fit with the casino driver's story that Elizabeth had ridden the bus alone to Memphis. Did Chris follow her? Was she abducted by a stranger in Memphis? How did she end up in the Tennessee River? He would have a slew of questions for Chris to answer this afternoon.

Chris was sitting in trigonometry class trying to concentrate on the teacher's lecture. His mind was on Beth and the findings in the river. He could not believe what his dad had read in the paper this morning -- that a body had been found and DNA tests were going to be done. Was it Beth? It was useless to try and concentrate with this latest news on his mind. She had been his girlfriend. And now something bad had happened to her. And they thought she was pregnant. Pregnant. How could that be? He was still thinking about that first time when the principal stuck his head into the classroom.

"We need to speak to Chris Daily, please for a few moments." Chris got out of his seat slowly and met the principal and the officer in the hallway.

"Chris, this is Officer Wayne Scott with the Tennessee Bureau of Investigation. He wants to ask you a few questions in my office."

"Okay."

They walked silently to the office, and once inside, the TBI officer closed the door and motioned for Chris to be seated. The officer remained standing and moved directly in front of Chris, overshadowing him, assuming the posture of the aggressor.

"Now, Chris, we just want to ask you a few questions about your whereabouts the night before Beth disappeared."

"But I told you guys months ago about it. I was home all night studying for an exam."

"Yes, you told us. But your parents say that you went to your room after supper. And they did not see you again until you called them from Beth's house Saturday morning. Where were you all that time?"

"At home, studying. I went to my room around 7 p.m. I flunked the last trig exam. I couldn't afford to flunk another one and stay on the team."

"You studied on a Friday night?"

"Well, yes. I knew Beth and I could spend Saturday together.

103

Sometimes she and Crystal do stuff on Friday nights anyway, like girl stuff."

"So, what time did you go to bed?"

"Around 11:00."

"You studied for four hours?"

"No. I studied until 9:00, and then I played video games until 11:00."

"You didn't call Elizabeth before going to bed?"

"My dad was on the computer. Free dial up. He's so cheap. He hates to be interrupted."

"Okay. What about your cell phone?"

"It was run down from being off the charger at school all day."

"And you didn't call her that morning before you went over to her house. Why not?"

"I never had to call first. I hang out there all the time. Her parents are cool."

"Well, they aren't very happy with you now, are they?"

"No. I guess not. I swear I didn't know she was pregnant."

"Is the baby yours?"

"Yeah, I mean...I guess so."

"What do you mean, you guess?"

"Well, I was her first, and I don't think she was sleeping around."

"You don't think. But you don't know for sure?"

"I'm pretty sure. She told me she loved me."

"And you love her? That's why you told your buddies the night you had sex for the first time that she took the bait just like all the rest."

Chris' face turned pale.

"I did say that. But she really was becoming special to me. I wouldn't hurt her. Even if I had known. I didn't do anything to her. Honest."

"Is there anyone that can back up your story about studying all night? Maybe you called a friend? Maybe your mom came and told you goodnight?"

"No. I was alone all night."

"Chris, we are going to have to ask you to come to the station with us. We have some more questions for you to answer."

"But what about class? What about my parents? Don't I need a lawyer?"

105

"You're not under arrest yet, Chris. You can call your parents from the station, and they can bring whatever legal counsel you need with them. We need you to drive your car. Forensics will want to process it, even after all this time."

"Okay," Chris said, his voice barely audible. Tears were streaking his boyish face as he and the investigator left the building amidst the stares and whispers of Chris's peers and teachers. By this time, a reporter from WBBJ had pulled up to the curb in the station van. He trotted toward Chris with a camera. The investigator stood in front of Chris and assured the reporter that this was not the time or place for a story. As Chris covered his head with his jacket and ran to his car, the investigator strongly suggested to the reporter that he go elsewhere for his evening story until there was more news.

"Is Christopher Daily under arrest in the disappearance of Elizabeth Merriweather?"

"No comment at this time."

"Where is he going at this moment?"

"No comment."

"We heard that Elizabeth was suspected to be pregnant, is

that true?"

"No comment. Now if you please, I have work to do," the officer replied brusquely.

The officer got into his car and followed Chris's car out of the drive. The reporter rushed back to the van and followed. By nightfall, all of West Tennessee would know that Chris Daily was the prime suspect in the mysterious disappearance of the missing teen.

Chapter 9
Daughter of Levi

"Ana took to wife a daughter of Levi..."

Beth's eye still burned from the powerful blow that Catfish

had inflicted upon her. Without thinking, she had smarted off to

him about doing his own dirty laundry, because her back was

beginning to feel the strain of the gained weight. Her earlier

morning sickness had passed, and Catfish had been feeding her a

steady diet of bologna and crackers. Being uncomfortable in her

sweats had prompted the whole argument. April still had some cool

days, but her body temperature was running hot, and she was

sweltering in her winter clothes. She had begged Catfish to let her

go into town, but he would not hear of it. They had argued

considerably before she met the back of his hand across her face

with the reminder that he still had that knife. He sharpened it

nightly in front of her, and even though he had not tried to force

her into sex anymore, he forced her to sleep in his bed, tied to the

bedpost until morning to prevent her from leaving or causing him

bodily harm in his sleep.

After he hit her, he had opened his closet door and threw a

faded cotton dress at her. She looked stunned as she held it out

before her.

"Whose dress is this?"

"Shut up. Put it on and quit your whinin'. There's chores

to get done. I got spring plantin' to tend to. Them's some of Miz.

Jones' old rags. They might be a bit big, but judging by the way

you're puttin' on weight, it won't be long before you fill it out as

good as she did."

"Mrs. Jones? There was a Mrs. Jones? Where is she? She

leave you and this stinking place for civilization?" Beth yelled at

Catfish who was using the bathroom.

"I said shut up. That there is none of yer concern, Liza." Catfish

was standing in the doorway now. Beth was startled and half naked.

109

Her t-shirt lay in the floor. Her protruding belly was obvious. Up until now, she had managed to hide her growing baby from Catfish. She had been careful not to change in front of him, but their argument and her smarting eye had her off kilter.

Catfish's eyes wandered over her body, truth suddenly dawning on him. This was why she had run away from home. This meant more trouble for him. So far, he had managed to keep her out of the public's eye, but a new baby meant getting the midwife. A new baby meant diapers and extra food. But it would also mean an extra hand around the place in time. The wheels were still turning when he finally spoke.

"How long was you figurin' on keeping that youngun a secret?"

"What?"

"The baby. What are you, three, four months along? How long did you think you could keep it a secret? That's the real reason you ran away from home. Got your little behind in trouble. Your parents didn't know, did they?"

"No. I was going to Memphis for an abortion. I chickened out."

110

"So that's what you was a doin'. Gonna kill that baby. Now ain't that lowdown. And you call me white trash."

"I said I couldn't do it."

"Now what ya gonna do Liza? Me and you just gonna have us a little family now huh?"

"I would be home now if you hadn't kidnapped me."

"But you can't go home now. Your family will disown you. You're better off here."

"Do I have a choice?"

"No, I reckon ya don't. We'll get Momma Loraine to midwife when the time comes. I reckon we can use another hand around here. Always wanted a lil Cat." Beth did not comment, but she loathed the thought of Phineas Jones being a father to her child. "I'm a goin' into town for some milk and bread. You best have my overalls washed and hung out by the time I get back. And clean up around here. This place ain't fittin' for no youngun. Don't sass me no more, Liza. You got to learn your place in the home. You got to learn who is the king of this castle. And seein' as you're in the family way, you might as well start learning to please a man instead of just keeping his sheets warm."

111

Catfish took the truck keys out of his pocket and headed for the front door. "I'll be back in a couple hours, Mizzus Jones."

She watched his truck head down the steep drive and out of sight. She knew if the laundry wasn't done when he returned there would be a steep price to pay. She didn't want to put the baby in harm's way again. Beth picked up his dirty socks, his underwear, two pairs of filthy overalls, and her sweat pants, t-shirt, and dirty underwear. She had long since stopped wearing the bra that was way too tight. She loaded them in a plastic storage tub, threw in the bottle of generic detergent, and headed down to the riverside to scrub the clothes. At least the weather was milder now, and the cold Buffalo River water wouldn't numb her feet and hands.

She made her way over the rocky terrain. The sun was shining, and the trees were beginning to bud along the riverbank. A sea of spring color surrounded her. The birds had come back to roost and were singing, and bright green grass was beginning to fill in the muddy areas of the yard. Once she was beyond the old trailer, the landscape was a pastoral scene straight from one of her childhood story books.

She was startled in her thoughts by something that ran out

of the bushes and brushed against her leg. She could not see what it was for the basket of clothes in her arms. She threw the basket down in surprise, making the orange tabby cat scamper away. It was a large, beautifully marked tabby with just a hint of white under his chin. Beth wondered how he had made his way out to her in this wilderness. Did he belong to Catfish? Where had the cat been all during the winter? She stooped to pet the animal, but it scampered away. Still, it had brushed her leg. It might not be as wild as she thought.

The months of imprisonment and terror had left Beth emotionally bankrupt. Surviving from one day to the next was her goal, and she had found little pleasure in the passage of time. She had grown bitter from the consequences of her youthful choices, and had decided that this was her deserved punishment--life with Phineas. She cradled her stomach. This baby did nothing to deserve these consequences. This baby had no choice but to move within the realm of its mother's choices. This thought saddened her. She watched as the cat turned to her as if to ask what was wrong.

Slowly she followed with small, careful steps--no sudden moves. She wanted to hold the cat, to cuddle it close to her and

113

bury her face in it, and cry into its orange fur. She wanted to feel

the warmth of life again. She wanted to feel something besides

hatred and confusion. The cat trotted several yards downstream,

stopping each time to see if Beth was following, its golden eyes

winking and urging her on. They rambled past large limestone

outcrops along the riverbed. They rambled past overhanging trees

that were just beginning to bud. The sun was shining warm upon

Beth's face, and she was actually beginning to enjoy the feel of the

breeze upon her pale skin. The thin cotton outlined her pregnant

form as it was swept around her petite body by the wind. Her

bobbed blonde hair lifted gently here and there.

For one brief moment Beth was free. She held her arms out

like a ballet dancer and twirled, letting the cotton dress swirl around

her. She closed her eyes, and she was home. She was back in her

warm, safe room. She was dancing to Britney Spears, and the world

was right. The cat sat on a rock and licked its paws, and then

growing bored with the dance, mewed loudly to garner her

attention. Then it hopped off the backside of the rock and

disappeared.

Elizabeth ran toward the rock. Down below was a sandy

114

short beach. She caught sight of the orange tail as it disappeared beneath the upturned silver canoe. A canoe! For the first time in months, Beth dared to think of escape. Her first thought was to jump into the canoe and never look back. She ran toward the canoe. The closer she got, the more noise she heard coming from underneath--loud, insistent mewing. She got on her knees and bent to peer into the darkness. She lifted the canoe a bit to let some light in, and was surprised to find the orange tabby on its side with five kittens hungrily searching for their dinner.

"Oh you dear thing. You're a mama. You wanted me to find them. You must be starving. I'll bring you back some food in a bit." Beth had completely forgotten the load of laundry by the wayside. She sat and stared at the amazing miracles of life as she contemplated her own impending motherhood. *A good mother takes care of her babies, protects them. I have to get out of here, no matter what. I have to make a plan.*

The mama cat who had been content to lie back and let the babies suckle twitched, then suddenly shot out of the canoe straight as an arrow past Beth. The cat landed on its feet, clawing and wrestling with something in the grass a few feet away. Beth's eyes

115

widened as she stood up for a better view. The snake was striking

and missing. It had the familiar rattle on of its tail that Beth had

seen on True Grit. The cat hissed and clawed and pounced, each

time jumping out of the reach of the snakes' powerful jaws. Beth

wanted to cover her eyes, but couldn't. She wanted to run, but was

planted firmly by the canoe as if protecting the kittens. She was

horrified with the scene unfolding. Then, it was as if the snake knew

it had met its match. It suddenly retreated toward the waters and

swam away, with the mama cat watching, her chest heaving from

the exertion. The rattlesnake would have to look elsewhere for his

dinner today.

Shaken, Beth watched the snake swim off downstream. She

shuddered as she thought about the many times she had come to

the river. But it had been wintertime. The thought of poisonous

snakes had never occurred to her. This was a new fear, one she was

unwilling to face. The baby moved inside her, sensing Beth's

agitation. She knew she would have to get the clothes clean. She

would just have to be more careful. It had to have been at least an

hour since Catfish had left, and the clothes had not been washed.

She would have to hurry.

Beth ran back up the riverbank. She cut across the path by which she'd come, trying to cut off some time. How long had she been down by the river? She didn't know. She was thinking of the laundry basket ahead when something stopped her cold--new dirt, the length of a plot. Something had been buried here over the winter...or someone. A new horror dawned in Beth's mind, Mrs. Jones! Had she stumbled on Inetha's grave? Waves of nausea swept over her, and she threw up in the grass. She could not catch her breath. The panic was overwhelming. *Mrs. Jones is dead, and no one knows. This is an unmarked grave--no stone, no flowers. Who else could it be?*

He would kill her too if he got the chance. Visions of him sharpening the knife each night raced across her mind. He would kill her, and no one would be the wiser. Her family already thought she was dead. If she tried to run, and he caught her, he would carve her like a Christmas turkey, she was sure. She had to get those clothes washed and on the line before he returned--before he suspected anything. She could not let him know what she had discovered. She had to act naturally. How she was going to do that, she did not know. But she had to get those clothes to the river before he returned.

117

She made it to the basket and ran to the water's edge. A quick scan of the water and the beach around her for snakes assured her she was okay. At this moment, the most evil snake was Catfish. She had to avoid his venom at all cost. Hurriedly she scrubbed the overalls first, making sure she scrubbed the knees and ankles where they dragged the red earth. She scrubbed furiously and fast as if she were trying to scrub out the sins of the world. She scrubbed as if her very life depended upon the cleanliness of the overalls. She prayed under her breath:

"Oh God, I know I did wrong. I know I made this mess...but oh God...I need your help. I need a miracle."

Then, she hung her head and cried as the green river rolled on past. She prayed as she had never prayed before; desperately she groaned and cried out to God to help her in our hour of need. It was in this sacred moment that Elizabeth found grace in the eyes of her Creator. She could not see the future that lay ahead, but He could. His heart heard the plea of this little woman-child. He would not turn His back on such a broken and repentant heart. Her head was still bowed, her eyes still firmly closed, when finally the muddy stain lifted from the fabric and faded from view. God had carried her sin as far from her as the east is from the west--to be

remembered no more.

Chapter 10

Pharaoh's Curse

"Death comes on wings to he who enters the tomb of a Pharaoh..."

April 2006

It was nearly noon when Catfish pulled out of the E.W.

James parking lot. He had lingered longer in the store than he had

meant to, but there was still time to get a bite of dinner at the

Dinner Bell before heading back. He made his way into the

restaurant and spotted Poke at his usual table. He also noted a few

strangers seated at a table nearby. They had guns strapped around

their waist. He nodded at them politely as he eased into his seat

next to the window.

Although recently remodeled, the Dinner Bell still held

most of its rural charm. The ceiling was plastered with old license plates from many different states. New bright red curtains had been hung, and the owner had finally gotten an all-you-can-eat buffet, which was only available on the weekends for the low price of $6.95. A television had been added in the far corner of the room and was tuned to noonday news. Even the bathrooms had been remodeled to reflect a more modern flair, although Catfish wondered as he soaped his hands why the men's room would need a double sink. Only women went to the powder room in droves. Men did their business and got out.

"What's with the firepower?" he asked Poke. The waitress made her way over with a glass of sweet tea for Catfish.

"What'll it be today, Cat, the usual?"

"You know it, gal. And then I'll need a takeout order later."

"Fiddler coming right up with hushpuppies and vinegar slaw."

"Oh, them boys is from the TBI. They been down at Perryville dragging the river most of the morning. Guess they is headin' back to Nashville takin' the scenic route."

"Draggin' the river? Fisherman drown or somethin'?

"Naw, they found a backpack that belonged to that girl that disappeared back the first of the year..."

"They did? They thinkin' she jumped?"

"Don't know. Them boys ain't said much. What you doin' in town today?"

"Needed some beer and toilet paper."

Catfish raised the glass of iced tea to his lips. Poke saw the glimmer of gold on his finger about the same time Catfish realized that he had it on.

"Nice chunk o' gold on yer finger there. You strike it rich at the Horseshoe?"

"Yeah, I had a run a luck. Good thang too. With the new baby on the way."

Poke's eyes widened. "New baby. What the...?"

"Yep, bout time me and the missus carried on the family name, dontcha think?"

"Well, youn's ain't gettin' no younger. But I thought she was too sickly."

"I reckon the good Lord has smiled on us. She's a takin' it easy. I don't let her get out none. Don't want nothin' happenin' to her or the baby. Finally gonna get me that big strappin' boy."

"You old dog you. Don't you reckon you oughta bring her into town and let the doc check her out."

"Mama Lorraine will be a seein' to her. We is fine. I reckon babies come into the world every day without a doctor's help."

"I guess you're right, Cat. Man, yore days of freedom is over."

"I just about got enough cash to start buildin' that stick built home we been wantin'. Then I'm a gonna get outta the business, if ya know what I mean."

"You can't do that. What's us good old boys gonna do for fun then?"

"Reckon you'll have to take over the business if it means that much to ya. I got a family to raise."

Poke let out a roaring laugh that made the investigators look up from their plates.

"What's so funny 'bout that, you old coot?"

"Nothin' Cat. Nothin'"

The waitress returned with the steaming plate of fish, fries, and hushpuppies, and the conversation stalled as Catfish plowed into his lunch. Poke studied the ring on Cat's finger with great interest. There was the imprint of a bird-- an eagle, or falcon with its wings spread looking over an ancient figure on a throne. That was no ordinary ring. He wondered just how Catfish had come by it. He doubted Catfish would have picked out something with those eccentric details for himself. That Catfish was something else all right. He wondered if they would name the baby Phineas, Jr.

"Hey Callie, give me an order o' catfish and fries to go would ya."

"You got it, Cat."

"Got to keep her strength up. She's a eatin' for two now." He winked at Poke.

The investigators had finished their meal, left a generous tip, and were heading out the door. Catfish looked toward the door as it shut behind them. So the investigation was back open. He would have to be on the lookout for anyone snooping into his business. Poke was about the only one who ever visited, and he had been careful to meet him down riverside, claiming Inetha had to be kept from the secret of the marijuana trading. Yep, it was getting a bit too close to home for comfort. And now his pride had caused him

124

to boast of the baby. He probably should have kept that to himself as well, but he would explain that away in due time. He could always say Inetha left him with the baby, and he found him a pretty nursemaid and housekeeper to tend him. He would deal with that later. He paid for the fish, grabbed a toothpick, and waved off Poke.

"We playin' Poker later this week?"

"We always do. We been missin' ya. Figured you done got too high and mighty with the high rollers to hang with us."

"Nah, just busy gettin ready for plantin'. Need me a tractor instead o' that old tiller."

"I hear ya. We'll be lookin' for ya then."

Catfish had just left the Dinner Bell and headed back toward home. He was thinking about the investigators and the search of the river. He would do whatever it took to keep Liza hid. He could not go to prison for kidnapping, or worse yet, murder. He was already in over his head, not to mention the rings he'd stolen from Frankie. He should never have taken them. Frankie should never have called him white trash either. Maybe he should try to

125

fence the stolen artifacts himself. But he figured as soon as he did, Ace, whoever he was, would come out of the woodwork wanting his property. Ace had no way of finding him, he knew. But that would be just his luck. He glanced down at the golden ring on his finger. He wondered what it was worth. He wondered how one went about fencing ancient artifacts.

His eyes were diverted from the road. The sun was glinting off the gold into his eyes. Suddenly something very large and heavy hit the windshield with such force that it cracked all the way across. Catfish was startled and jerked the wheel. The truck fishtailed, hit some loose gravel, and began spinning out of control. Catfish caught the light of the water glancing off the river below. The truck was perilously close to the edge of the road and about to go over the ravine and crash into the green waters of the Buffalo. His heart was pounding in his throat. He yanked the wheel in the opposite direction, the truck hitting an outcrop of limestone on the left side of the road. The truck rattled as it was scraped by the rock. It swerved and headed back toward the river. He corrected the wheel and fishtailed again. Finally, Catfish managed to get control of the wheel and bring the truck to a stop on a wide flat area just past the

126

river.

His hands were sweaty and shaking as he rolled to a stop. His mouth was dry as he cursed the luck that nearly took his life. What was that huge bird that had hit his windshield? He looked in his rearview mirror, but could see nothing lying in the road. He ran his hand through his hair. Whatever it was had come pretty near killing him. The bags of groceries had hit the floorboard. Cans of potted meat and chili were rolling around. He was amazed to see that the Styrofoam container that held Liza's lunch was still sitting on the seat beside him. He reached for his to-go cup of iced tea and took long drags on the straw. At least the truck would still run. Good Old Faithful. Maybe he would forget about the Navigator after all. Was this was nature's way of quelling the greed that had begun taking hold of him? He would have to find a way to get rid of the rings. The heat was getting too intense. He had enough to worry about with a baby on the way. There was a crop to get planted. This would be his last and biggest crop. Of course he would have to find a new buyer. But he was certain that was only a small formality. There were plenty of buyers in the big city. Once he took care of that little matter life would be good again. Just him

127

and Liza and P.J., living the royal life in the royal kingdom. There would be nothing holding him back from the good life then.

Catfish wiped the sweat from his brow and managed to calm his racing heart. He flipped the radio on. That would calm his nerves a bit. He put the truck in gear and carefully pulled back out onto the road. A radio station out of Nashville broadcast the story. A body had been found by the divers at Decaturville, along with a pair of sunglasses and one of her flip-flops. The name of the victim had not been released pending the results of DNA testing, but it could possibly be a 17-year-old runaway that disappeared last January from her home in Jackson, Tennessee. The girl was believed to be pregnant. Foul play was suspected. *A body? They found a body?*

Catfish turned off the radio. He peered out the dirty, cracked windshield and across the yard. He was not sure who the divers had discovered in the river, but he was certain it was not Liza Beth. She was reaching into a nearby basket for a pair of his overalls. Her long, blonde hair had been crudely cut into a bob, and she had a purple bruise under her left eye. She should not have sassed him. A woman should know her place in the home.

128

129

Chapter 11

Words of Hope

"Come let us deal wisely with them..."

Without sufficient physical evidence linking Chris to Beth's

disappearance, the police had nothing to hold him on, so after

extensive questioning with him and his legal counsel and his

parents, the police let Chris walk free with the condition that he not

leave town. Beth's parents were furious with the latest

developments, certain that Chris had knowledge of their daughter's

whereabouts. Beth's father was waiting outside the jail as Chris and his parents exited the station.

"What did you do to her? Where is she...what did you do with my daughter...." His face was purple, his hand doubled into a fist as he charged toward them.

Chris's father rushed to guard his son from any blows that Mr. Merriweather might inflict.

"Hold it John! I know you're upset."

"Upset! Upset...how would you feel if it were your daughter, Bob? Where is Beth, Chris...where is she?"

"I...uh...I...I'm sorry. I had nothing to do with this..."

"Please, just leave us alone. Let us go home. The publicity of this is ruining my son's life. Just let us go home." Chris's mother pleaded.

"Ruining your life? What about my life, my family's lives, my daughter's life? What about that, huh?"

"John, please. We loved Beth. Chris loved Beth. Please..."

By this time an on-duty policeman who had been watching made his way to the group and pulled John aside.

"Mr. Merriweather, we can't hold him. There's no evidence.

131

Just please, let them by. Come inside, and we will discuss the next step of the investigation."

"The next step? Where do we go from here? He's guilty. I know he is."

"Now, you know that the accused is innocent until proven guilty. Besides, there may be something, someone we've overlooked. Come inside, and we'll talk."

Reluctantly, John followed the detective back inside the police station. His steps were weary. All he wanted at this moment was justice for his daughter. He had come to terms with the fact that she was probably dead, as well as their grandchild. But he wanted her found. He wanted closure. He owed it to Elizabeth. As her father, he owed her the decency of a final resting place. He would not rest until Beth was brought home.

"What about the reporter that spread that garbage about our daughter's body being found?"

"Unfortunately, there's nothing we can do to prosecute him. He was overeager. His facts were false. But it's a matter for the civil courts. Your lawyer can advise you how to proceed with that. If it were me, I'd sue for every penny I could get. But even at that, I'm sure your daughter's life is worth far more to you. I just wish we had more to go on."

"My wife was hysterical when she heard that report. The mental anguish it caused was devastating."

"The media does tend to go overboard. Wish there was more we could do to protect you guys from it. I suggest you try to keep your family out of the limelight as best you can for a few weeks. They will move on to something else before long."

"It's not that I don't appreciate the coverage and the attention brought to the case, but false reporting is inexcusable."

"I agree totally. Have a seat. You want some coffee, soda?"

"Coffee's fine."

"Now, as you know, the river search came up empty handed as far as a body goes. No body, no evidence to hold Chris on. On the other hand, no body means that we cannot prove she's dead, which means there is hope that she may well still be alive."

"Alive? You really think there is hope of that? Wouldn't we have some new leads by now? Doesn't the backpack indicate that she drowned in the river?"

"Initially, it would seem that way. But what if someone just wanted it to appear that she drowned. What if Beth wanted it to appear that way?"

"Why would she do that? Why would she cause her mother and me such heartache? She is bound to know how hurt we are. No, I don't think she would hurt us that way."

"You don't think the shame of the pregnancy would cause her to run away and fake her death?"

"I would hope that she knows we love her enough to forgive anything bad she had done. She wouldn't be the first girl to have gotten in trouble."

"No, she wouldn't. But she was such a good student. Such a popular student. She probably felt all her dreams and hopes were shattered. It's not uncommon for pregnant teens to become runaways. It is uncommon for them not to turn up after all this time. A lot of times they show up at the hospital when it's time for the baby to be born. There's still that hope."

"I hadn't thought of that. But where could she be hiding? How is she living? What about medical care for her and the baby?"

"We are still checking all the states' medical and obstetrical clinics, but it is a slow process. So far we've turned up nothing.

Since the initial search was concentrated in Jackson and Memphis, and the backpack was found in the Tennessee River, the search has now shifted gears to include Middle Tennessee. The TBI has been called in to help with the interviews and the search in those counties east of here. The terrain is extremely rural. There's any number of hiding places. And just to let you know, we aren't necessarily looking for a body."

"That is encouraging, but after all these months, I'm afraid to get my hopes up, you understand."

"I understand, totally."

"I take it you did not get any new information from Chris."

"No. If Chris is involved, he is very clever. But if he is, we will catch him eventually."

"You can't arrest him for statutory rape or something like that?"

"With Beth almost 18, it is unlikely that charge would stick. There is no proof that sexual congress actually took place without semen samples or other DNA."

"What about the pregnancy test?"

"It proves that Beth was or is pregnant. The urine sample

135

proved that it is Beth's DNA. It does not indicate paternity. There's no way to determine that without samples from Beth and the baby."

"I see. So, without Beth, there's no way Chris can be held?"

"No. Sometimes in cases like this, we arrest the suspect on other charges so that we can hold them until we get further evidence for a murder case. For instance, if Chris was in possession of something of value of Beth's, then we could charge him with theft and hold him for two or three days. But then, we would most likely have to release him until his day in court unless further evidence turned up, or Chris caved under questioning."

"What about that case out in California? They arrested him, didn't they?"

"If you recall, he was a free man until the bodies washed ashore. The police followed him, traced his calls, and hassled him, but until the bodies turned up, he was free to come and go as he pleased. But the tapes of his phone calls is what eventually got him convicted. And don't think we aren't watching Chris very closely. He is very much a person of interest in this case, Mr.Merriweather."

"If I could just have five minutes alone with him, I could

crack him. I know I could..."

"Please, John, please leave the detective work to the professionals. You could do more harm than good. And then we might never find your daughter."

"I guess you're right...it's ...just so...hard." John buried his face in his hands and cried.

The investigator put a hand on John's shoulder and tried to comfort him.

"We're doing all we can. Now go home to your wife. We will call you if there are any new developments. And I would advise against any contact with the media."

"Thank you for all your help."

"You bet. We'll call you."

John left the police station encouraged by the investigator's words of hope. Could it be possible that Elizabeth was just a runaway, scared to face her parents and the consequences of her choices? The pregnancy complicated things, but it wasn't something John and his wife would shun Beth for; she had to know that. They would do everything in their power to support her if she would just come home. It wasn't the end of the world. If she were alive, someone somewhere had to know of her whereabouts. She would have to have food and lodging. Money talks. He and Carolyn would up the reward. If Beth was out there, they would find her. If she were dead, then God help the person who was responsible.

Seventy-five miles away their daughter was sitting at a rickety metal dinette eating greasy, cold catfish and trembling at the thought of all she had discovered. Catfish had returned in a foul mood and muttered something about wrecking the truck after a buzzard hit the windshield. She knew she shouldn't hate, but she found herself wishing that Catfish had actually been killed in the wreck, instead of surviving and making her life this living hell. Catfish sat over in the dirty recliner and sharpened his knife, stopping only to swig warm beer from the can and make crude belching noises. Yes, she would have given anything at that moment if the buzzard that hit his truck were here to peck out his eyes. And then in shame, she repented. She knew the wilderness was beginning to turn her into a wild beast no better than her captor.

Chapter 12

Learnin' the Ropes

May 2006

Catfish thought she had turned out to be a fair-to-middlin'
housewife. She took to gardening right well. They had planted
corn, beans, potatoes, peas, and tomatoes. She hadn't liked hoeing
much, hadn't liked the blisters on her pretty white hands. But once
he had smacked her for whining she had toughened up
considerably. The Jones's were from strong stock. The mother of
his boy had better learn to buck up. He had rigged a siphon system
from the fifty gallon drum to water the garden, but the rain had
been scarce, so he and Liza had to haul five gallon buckets of water
from the river to fill the drum. Once the vegetables came in, Liza
would get a crash course on canning and cooking. All in due time.

140

"Liza, now that the weather's warmin' up, it's time you learned the art of fishin'. Get yer shoes on. We goin' down to the river."

Liza knew better than to smart off to him, although the last thing she wanted to do was handle all those slimy fish. Catfish's gruff voice snapped her back to reality.

"Get your tail in gear! We got work to do."

They drove the old truck over the bumpy terrain down to the water's edge. Catfish had placed two large coolers on the back of the truck, one to hold his beer and soda, and the other to hold the fish they would catch. He also threw a large net over the side of the truck, but no fishing poles or tackle.

"Ready to earn yer keep? I bet a city girl like you never been fishin'."

"We used to go up to Paris Landing some weekends." She had fond memories of fishing trips to Paris Landing with her mom and dad. But this was different. Her daddy would fish off the boat while she swam or sunbathed with her feet propped on the boat rail. Her mom had always packed a cooler of sandwiches and cold drinks to enjoy. Those days were long gone now.

141

"Well, I bet ya never fished this way." Catfish pulled the heavy net out from the back of the truck.

"Ever fished with a net before?"

"Can't say as I have," she replied disinterested.

"Gotta know where to cast. That's the key."

Beth wondered if this method really worked, but marveled as Catfish swung the net up and out into a high arc over the water. The net seemed to hang momentarily in mid-air, and then float gracefully down into the pungent water and disappear. Then Catfish popped open a beer and sat down on the riverbank to wait.

An hour later, Catfish got to his feet and made his way over to the net. He carefully pulled up the tethered edge and began pulling the net toward him with steady, skilled tugs. Once the net made it to land, he stuck his hand down among the fish to survey his catch.

"A couple of good sized cat, three or four bream, and a couple of yellow perch. Not a bad start. Bring me the cooler." Beth grabbed the cooler from the tailgate of the truck and set it in front of him. He dumped the fish over into it, and carried it back to the river and cast again. He popped another beer and returned to his spot in the shade.

"Gonna have some good eatin' tonight," he said between sips.

"I don't know how to cook fish," Beth replied dryly.

"High time you learned how to, and how to clean 'em too."

Beth closed the lid on the cooler and sat down on it. Her body was beginning to get cumbersome to her. She was thinking about the unpleasant task of cleaning the fish when something brushing against her leg startled her. Remembering the rattlesnake encounter, Beth jumped to her feet with a squeal.

"What is it, girl?" Catfish asked.

"Oh, you scared me Rascal," Beth said to the kitten as she bent to scoop up the orange kitty.

"My how you've grown. Where are your sisters? Where's your mama, huh?"

Catfish wrinkled his nose in disgust and spat a wad of tobacco over into the weeds.

"Where'd that come from? You say there's more?"

"I found them…" And then she stopped. She didn't want Catfish to know she'd found the canoe. And she sure didn't want

143

him to know she'd discovered the grave. "I found them down here the other day when I came to do the wash."

"You been feedin' em ain't ya. We don't need no more mouths to feed, Liza. Don't never feed strays."

He had gotten to his feet by now. Before Beth had time to reply he had jerked the kitten by the scruff of her neck out of Beth's hands. Her eyes widened in horror as he reared his arm back and slung the helpless kitten as far out into the river as he could. Beth screamed in horror and ran at him, catching him off guard. He stumbled, but caught himself before he fell. He grabbed her roughly and held her arms to keep her from clawing at his face.

"You killed him! Why did you have to kill him?" she screamed.

"If you know what's good for you," His breath was ragged from the struggle. "If you know what's good for you, you'll sit down and shut up. And if you don't, that kitten won't be the only thing tossed in."

His expression had changed from relaxed fisherman to crazed killer. The transformation was swift and complete. He released her, and Beth made a desperate attempt to hold back the

144

sniffing and shaking as she weakly made her way back to the cooler where she sat for the next two hours trembling and praying. Finally, Catfish pulled the net in one more time and announced it was time to get back to the house.

They rode in silence back up the hill, and once they reached the trailer, Catfish got out and pulled the cooler over to a spot in the shade where an old wooden table sat.

"Go get a couple of them five gallon buckets and bring 'em here. And hurry up!" He turned the buckets upside down and ordered Beth to sit.

"Now pay attention. This ain't brain surgery." Catfish pulled the largest catfish from the cooler. He knocked it in the head with the heavy handle end of the knife he had brought with him and laid it on its side on the table. First he scored the fish with small cuts on both sides near the back of the head. He inserted his thumb in the fish's mouth with one hand and grabbed the skin at the score and peeled it all the way down the fish on one side. Then Catfish turned the fish over and peeled the other side clean before chopping the head off and throwing it to his dog Fetch who had wandered up. He made one final long cut the length of the fish's

145

belly and scooped the intestines and vital organs out with the blade of the knife.

"And there you have it. Ready for the fryin' pan."

His movements were swift and skilled. Beth's stomach churned at the thought of Catfish's promises on the day they met. She knew he would make good on them if she ever crossed him again.

Chapter 13

This Do in Remembrance

Chris put his arm around Crystal's shoulder and smiled for

the camera as Crystal's mother took a quick picture of them before

they headed over to the high school. The two had become close

friends during their months of tragedy as Crystal championed Chris'

innocence to the student body. Crystal knew in her heart that Chris

could not have murdered Beth; some other evil had taken her from

them that winter night. All they could do now was hope and pray

for her return and continue on with life as best they could. Her

efforts had paid off, and the student body had once again embraced

Chris as their own. They smiled weakly for the camera.

"Don't you two look stunning tonight," remarked Crystal's

mom.

Crystal's hair was pulled back in a tight French braid. Loose tendrils of auburn framed the small pixie face, and she smiled broadly while lifting the hem of her purple satin gown and tiptoed to the car, careful not to let her heels dig into the lawn.

"You clean up good Chris."

"Actually I was thinking the same thing about you, Crys."

"You both look marvelous. Have a good time, dear," she said as she pecked Crystal on the cheek. "Be home by midnight. And behave yourselves."

"Don't worry, Mrs. Barnes, I'll have her home early." Chris wondered if Mrs. Barnes was worried about letting her daughter go out with someone under such a great cloud of suspicion. He wanted to reassure her he was not a monster. He wanted to let her know that there was no way he would hurt Crystal.

Then, Mrs. Barnes, seeing the worry in Chris's face, drew him to her and hugged him tight.

"I know she will be safe with you, son. I know you had nothing to do with Beth's disappearance. I knew it from Day One. Now, go have fun."

After they got in the car, Chris turned to Crystal. He

149

couldn't believe what had just happened. Mrs. Barnes was smiling and waving good-bye to them as they drove away.

"How can your mom be so certain that you're safe with me after all that's happened?"

"Chris, mom has a way of knowing things that other people don't. Trust me, if she thought for one minute you were involved in Beth's disappearance, I wouldn't be here. She prays for you and your family every night when she prays for Beth and her family. I think that is what has gotten us this far."

"I wish my mom was a little more like her, then. Mom still questions me about that night. I can't believe she would suspect her own son." Crystal laid her hand over Chris's.

"We'll find her, Chris. And then everyone will know. We'll find her, and she'll tell us where she's been all these months."

"I wish I could believe that. But it's hard for me to hope for the fairytale ending. It's been so long."

"I know..." Crystal's voice trailed off as the car pulled into the parking lot of the high school. Chris came around the side of the mustang and opened the door. Crystal put her delicate arm in the crook of Chris's arm and together they held their heads high

150

and entered the gymnasium where they were met by a throng of teens in ball gowns and tuxedos.

Bright primary- colored balloons arched the entryway to the gymnasium, which had been transformed by many hours of labor into a giant ballroom. Lace topped tables were grouped around the outer edges of the dance floor with blue and yellow balloon centerpieces. Shiny confetti was strewn about on the floor and tabletops; a strobe light spun in mid-air from the ceiling. To the left were the buffet tables laden with finger foods, desserts, and punch. A huge banner graced the right wall that read, "Memories in the Making."

The Prom King and Queen's table was set on stage in a place of honor. Chris and Beth had been elected for the honors this year. Everyone agreed that Beth would hold the honor, and Crystal would hold her place by proxy. A large eight by ten photo of Elizabeth sat in a gold frame facing the audience surrounded by several low candles. Chris had to struggle to keep the tears back as he took his place at the table. Crystal dabbed at her eyes, but the tears refused to stay hidden.

"It's okay, Crys. You still look beautiful. Beth would be so proud to know you held her spot for her. I've got to get myself

together. There's something I have to do."

"What's that?" Crystal said, still sniffling.

"You'll see," he answered as he made his way to the microphone

at center stage.

"Attention, everyone. Welcome to North Side High

School, Prom 2006." Cheers and whistles erupted from the crowd

below. "Before we get started tonight with all the festivities, I, as

Prom King, have a special dedication for my Prom Queen,

Elizabeth Merriweather." His voice began to crack as he choked

back the emotion in his voice. Silence filled the hall.

"Beth, I know you're still with us. I know you're out there alive

somewhere. Please come home. Your friends miss you. I miss

you. We all love you, Beth. This is for you."

Chris nodded at the DJ who had been let in on the secret.

The soft music began as Chris urged the crowd to find someone

special to share the dance with. Crystal sat at the table behind Chris

with admiring tears brimming from her eyes as Chris began to sing

the words to "Miss You Like Crazy." When the song ended, there

was a half-second pause, and then thunderous applause erupted as

152

Chris returned to the table and held out his hand to Crystal. They made their way to the dance floor arm in arm. The d-jay, sensing a need for some relief from the tension, cued a fast paced song and announced jovially, "Let's get this party started!"

Tears flowed freely again on graduation day as the students filed to their seats leaving an empty seat for Elizabeth. Her name was called out with all the other seniors, even though she technically lacked nearly a whole semester of school. Beth's parents accepted her diploma on her behalf, along with the three scholarships she had been awarded and the various school awards. A representative from Union University made the presentation of the scholarships and informed the crowd and Beth's parents that the scholarships would stand awarded to her, and that if, for any reason, Beth did not use the scholarships, or choose to use them, John and Carolyn could decide on whom to bestow the funds at a later date.

When the final prayer was given, shouts of jubilation pierced the night and two hundred silk hats went flying up toward the evening sky, illuminated in their ascent by the stadium lights. Chris bent to pick his hat up from the ground, and with a deep sigh

153

he brushed the dirt from its tassel. Overwhelmed with all the emotions of the night's events, Chris mumbled in quiet reflection, "One of these should have been yours..."

155

Chapter 14
Hope Deferred
June 2006

In the weeks that followed the backpack discovery, John and

Carolyn managed to raise the reward amount to $250,000 by getting

a second mortgage on their home and selling some of their luxuries

like the fishing boat in the garage. John knew he would never be

able to enjoy fishing again anyway, and nothing was more important

than finding out what had happened to his little girl. Against the

advice of the police, they contacted the media and arranged to have

a press conference detailing the new reward.

"If anyone out there has information leading to the whereabouts of our daughter, Elizabeth Merriweather, please, please come forward. You can remain anonymous and still collect the reward if our daughter is found, dead or alive. We just want the information. Please, please help us find her. If you are holding her hostage, contact us to arrange for the ransom money to be delivered in exchange for our daughter. Elizabeth, if you are watching, we love you. We want you to come home. We want you and our grandchild. We don't care where you've been or what you've done. Just come home to us. We love you."

They were not prepared for the chaos that followed in June. Leads came pouring in from all over the country, and a few from outside the country, further raising the Merriweather's hopes that their daughter was, indeed, still alive. There were so many new leads that the police were having a hard time following up on them all. The hotline they had set up rang constantly. Each time it was someone claiming to have seen Elizabeth in their neighborhood, at a convenience store, hitch hiking through the mountains, or shopping for groceries. Volunteers were brought in to man the phones and take down crucial contact information so that the police could follow up each lead.

The investigator was brutally honest when he spoke to John about the case. He was not jubilant, as John expected, but rather somber.

"You realize that the money has brought out every crazy in the woodwork, don't you John. You may have slowed the investigation to a crawl."

"I don't see it that way. At least we're getting leads. Just because you guys have to do a bit of work to keep up, that's not my fault."

"John, we don't have the manpower to keep up the pace. As harsh as it sounds, your case is not our only case."

"What are you saying? That you won't follow up on these leads?"

"No, I'm not saying that. I'm saying that we will do our best, but we have other cases to work. Don't expect too much is all."

"I fully expect you to follow up on each and every lead as if it were the one to bring my girl home. Do you understand?"

"I understand. As long as you understand, John, that raising the reward money does not guarantee we'll find her."

158

"I'm fully aware of that. Now get back to work finding my daughter."

"There are at least three very promising leads I need you to be informed of, John. Two we can follow up on. The third is out of our jurisdiction. Out of the country even. There's a mountain of red tape involved. There's a chance your daughter might have been sold into a prostitution ring in the Caribbean. A tourist claims to have seen a young blonde fitting her description in the straw market in Montego Bay, Jamaica. She was obviously pregnant, and she fit the description. Her hair was braided, and she was soliciting tourists for sex and was in the company of a tall Rastafarian native wearing dreadlocks and a rainbow-colored toboggan. We have no jurisdiction in the British Isles, but we are considering sending a private investigative team down there under the auspices of tourism."

"I'm going. I have to go. Carolyn and I will get a flight out tomorrow."

"Don't go flying off on a whim, John. Let the professionals handle this."

"I can't just sit by and let my daughter be held captive on

159

some West Indies island. If it's her, I'm bringing her home."

"You will just attract more media attention John. It could scare her captors. You could be endangering her."

"Then I will just have to go undercover, won't I?"

"I can't say as I blame you John. You do what you have to do. But be careful. It's a different world. Take some protection with you. Take the professional team with you, John. You don't know what you're dealing with."

"Okay, you're right. Give me their contact info. I'll arrange for us all to go down together."

"The team is AriesOne. They have experience with investigating crimes like this. But they specialize in finding bodies. Either way, you're in good hands. I trust them. Give me a couple of days, John. We'll set it all up for you. If you must go, this will give you time to get your things together and get your business taken care of here."

"Fine. Let me know as soon as you have the arrangements. And while we're gone, I expect you to follow up on those other two leads, in case this doesn't pan out. We're going to find her. I can feel it. My daughter's not dead."

"I sincerely hope you do find her John. We all could use a happy ending to this one."

It was a balmy 85 degrees when AirJamaica touched down on the short Montego Bay runway on Memorial Day. The aquamarine Caribbean water rushed up to meet them, the Blue Mountains blurring past the windows as the plane screeched to a halt. Airport workers rolled temporary steps up to the doorway, and the passengers descended onto the airport pavement. John and Carolyn stepped off first, followed by three middle-aged men in short sleeves. They were greeted in the lobby by lovely ladies passing out Jamaican rum and dancing to the strains of Reggae.

"Welcome to Jamaica, mon," they nodded.

The airport was hot and sweaty, and they spent an hour waiting for their luggage. Finally they retrieved their baggage and made their way to an airport van that was to take them to their hotel. They passed vibrant flowering plants and palm trees that swayed in the breeze. Carolyn studied every face of every person she passed. It was a small island. She would scour every square inch of it if she had to. She would find the Rastafarian with the rainbow toboggan and dreadlocks down his back. She would find him. And then she

161

would find her daughter.

The van took rattled along the street. It wound its way along the bay, offering breathtaking views of the sunset that was upon them. They were behind a slow moving vehicle, but not for long. The driver honked his horn two short honks, and then proceeded to pass on the hill. Carolyn held her breath and prayed. The driver noticed her in his mirror.

"No worries, Mum. It's the way of life here. I get you there safe and sound Mum." But by the looks of the van, the obvious rusted dents in the front and back bumpers, Carolyn had to doubt his optimism. She was grateful when the van finally pulled up in front of their hotel. She had breathed diesel the entire way, and was feeling a bit nauseous from the reckless drive. John steadied her as they exited the van.

"Let's get checked in, hon. We'll start the search tomorrow."

"We have to find her John. We've come all this way. I can't face another disappointment."

"We'll find her, honey, we will." Then John turned to the three men that had arrived with them.

"We'd like to freshen up a bit, get cleaned up for supper.

How about we meet in the lobby at 6:00 to discuss our plan of action?"

"That will be fine, John. We want you to know we're going to do everything in our power to help you find Beth. If she is on the island, we will find her."

"I so appreciate your agreeing to help out with the search. Her mother and I are encouraged by this new lead."

"Never give up hope, John. We have seen some happy endings. You might just get your miracle."

"We do believe in miracles. We have hope in God. See you at 6:00."

They made their way to their ocean view room and unpacked. Carolyn had brought a week's worth of clothing with her, unsure of how long it might take to find her daughter. She sat down on the bed and faced the patio doors. She looked out toward the ocean. This was paradise. This was a place for honeymooners and vacationers. It was inconceivable to her that someone could have kidnapped her only child and brought her here to exploit her body. If that was truly the case, then what would they do to her when they realized she was pregnant? None of it fit. Still, there was

163

the lead that had come in. Was it a red herring? Had someone deliberately lured them to Jamaica to turn their attention away from the local search? Maybe it was someone else's little girl in trouble.

Ever since Elizabeth disappeared, Carolyn had grieved in her heart for any mother who had lost a child. This was truly the worst thing that could ever happen to a mother. Yet, it happened to one somewhere every day. She would never throw out a milk carton again without studying the faces of the missing children on the side. She would never pass a poster on a bulletin board again without poring over the pictures and saying a prayer for that family, that mother, that child. The plight of these mothers was now real to her. It was her battle now. She must find strength to face whatever lay ahead.

"John, did you ever think when Elizabeth was a tiny baby that we would ever face such an agonizing day as this?"

"No, honey. I never dreamed. No parent wants to think of this ever happening."

"I know that no one wants to believe their child is dead. But John, I just don't feel in my spirit that she is. I can feel her. At night when I close my eyes, I hear her calling out to me. She is alive

164

somewhere. Someone is keeping her from us. But she is alive. We cannot stop looking."

John sat down on the bed beside his wife. He placed an arm around her and pulled her close to him. He ran his hand through her blonde hair. He closed his eyes and pictured Elizabeth's blonde hair.

"She is a strong young woman like her mother. She will survive. Our grandchild will survive. We have to trust God to keep her safe. Be strong Carolyn. She's in God's hands. He is in control of our lives...and our daughter's life. We must cling to our faith in Him. Together we will make it."

Carolyn looked up at John with tears shining in her eyes.

"I don't know what people do who don't have God in their hearts to turn to, to lean on."

"Neither do I, honey. Neither do I."

Chapter 15

When I Became a Man

Over the last six months since Beth went missing,

Christopher Daily had done a lot of soul searching about his role in

his girlfriend's disappearance. No, he hadn't kidnapped her or

caused her bodily harm, but he had gotten her in trouble on that

night in November. He had tempted her to give in to him; he had

introduced her to alcohol and sex. Technically he was at fault. And the guilt that he carried with him on a daily basis began to eat away at his sanity. He had convinced her that he could be trusted. It was a lie he had told many times to many girls. If a girl was going to be that naive, then he was certainly not going to turn down a sure thing. But he hadn't counted on this turn of events. He felt ashamed and dirty. Why should he be allowed to go on about his daily life when Beth was dead, or out there suffering? *Where are you Beth? Why didn't you tell me? Where did you go?* And then other thoughts began to flood his mind, thoughts he could barely stand to entertain.

We made a baby together. I'm going to be a daddy, well I was going to be a daddy. What's happened to Beth and my baby? He wondered if it would have been a boy or a girl, and if it would have looked like him. *I'm too young to be a father. I have plans for my future. But what about Beth's future? What about our child's future?* They could have worked something out. He could have gotten a job. His parents and Beth's parents would have helped out. It wasn't the end of the world. It must have seemed like the end of the world to her. She must have been scared out of her mind. She must have been so ashamed. And she couldn't tell me. She couldn't tell anyone.

167

When Chris closed his eyes at night he saw Beth's face. He heard her calling out to him from some dark and shadowy void, which he prayed was not death. "Help me, Chris. Please help me. I'm so scared." He could see her tearful blue eyes. He could see her reaching out to him with one hand, the other hand cradling her bulging stomach. She had to be alive. She was so pretty. So young. She was out there somewhere. He missed her--her laugh, her smile, that sparkling, bubbly personality. Did he love her? He wasn't sure. He had not given their relationship a chance to bloom. He had crossed the boundaries of intimacy without so much as a second thought. He was too young to think about having a serious relationship. And sadly, he realized now, he was really too young for the intricacies of an intimate relationship with anyone. He knew that now. The fire that he had been playing with had caused irreparable damage to all their lives. And even though he was off the hookay as far as the law was concerned, he was still guilty. Guilty as charged. The weight of his guilt felt like a thousand pounds of iron lying over his heart. And for the first time in his life, Chris Daily lay upon his bed and wept true tears of sorrow.

"Dear God, It's me, Chris. God, I know that You're not

happy with how I've been living my life. I know that I have been wild and loose and testing my limits. I've gone against everything my parents have tried to teach me about being a good person, about doing the right thing, about being a Christian. I know I've been raised in a Christian home. But God, I've never asked Jesus into my heart. I've never asked for forgiveness for the wrong things I've done. Oh God. I am so sorry for what has happened. I'm sorry for all the wrong I've done, the drinking, the partying, the sex. I'm sorry for lying to all those girls I went with, and for taking away their innocence. I'm especially sorry for hurting Beth. God help us find her. Protect her and the baby. I know she's out there. She's scared God. Help her to find her way home. Jesus I believe in You and Your death on the cross. I believe in the power of your blood to save me. I ask Your forgiveness. I ask You to save me from my sin. I ask you to come into my heart tonight, and live there. I want to be a better man. I want to know what it is to have peace. God help me. Help us all. In the name of Jesus Christ our Lord, Amen."

As soon as the words had escaped his lips, Chris felt a calm in his spirit. His breathing slowed, and his tears stopped flowing. A strange warmth began to fill his being as the peace of God

169

flooded over him. This was a feeling like no other he had ever experienced--a feeling that no alcohol could ever elicit. It was a feeling that no physical connection could duplicate. Nothing that Chris had ever encountered in his eighteen years felt as free and as wonderful as this fountain of grace that was flowing in and through him at this moment. His manhood was not defined by his casual intimate encounters, but by his willingness to accept responsibility for his guilt. And accept the grace afforded to him by Christ's sacrifice on the cross. It was on this hot summer night, in his own little bedroom in his parent's home in Jackson, Tennessee that Christopher Scott Daily put away the idols of his youth and the sins that had so easily beset him. Not only had Chris, this night, become a Christian, but he had, indeed, become a man. And from this night on, Chris knew that his life would never be the same.

Chapter 16

Thy will be done, Lord

It had been a miserable month in Jamaica for the

Merriweathers. Every morning after breakfast, John and Carolyn

gathered stacks of fliers, donned their walking shoes, and set out to

comb the island for signs of their daughter. Every morning and

evening the search team briefed them on the day's findings--or lack

of them. Every day Carolyn grew more and more despondent and

John more stoic. From the very first day on the island it was

apparent that this was going to be no easy challenge, despite the smallness of the island. Their search had stretched from Montego

Bay all the way to the far end of the island in Kingston, with

Kingston being a primary focus due to its size and population. No

one had even the slightest information that could lead to Beth.

Most of the islanders approached would just shrug their

shoulders and look away. Unemployment was at an all-time high for

Jamaica, and they relied heavily on their income from tourists to

support the island. No one was willing to jeopardize their

international traffic to help the pitiful couple from Tennessee, no

matter how much they sympathized with their plight. Carolyn also

learned-- much to her dismay-- the rainbow colored toboggans were

sold at every market on the island. Everyone wore them. And a

large percentage of the native islanders wore their hair in

dreadlocks. What Carolyn thought was a fantastic description

turned out to be a nightmare. Her heart leapt every time she saw

one of the brightly colored hats. She immediately scanned the

surrounding tourists for petite, young blondes. Her interest was

greatly piqued by the ones that were pregnant. Now that she was

looking for a pregnant girl, every young woman on the beach

seemed to have that familiar pouch in her stomach.

173

The search team had combed the island for any new land disturbances. They had probed the beaches and caves and most likely spots for burial of a body. They had combed construction sites and landfills. They had walked the streets of Kingston with pictures, and at times even offered money for information. They had knocked on so many doors that news had spread to neighboring communities of them before they even arrived, and the residents would not even come to the door. The grueling days turned into weeks with little reward. Unless John and Carolyn could raise more funds to finance the search, the team would have to return to the U.S. empty handed. But John was not ready to give up on the search.

"Maybe we should head up into the mountain regions today--up near Christiana."

"Actually, there is a spot, a small community known as Green Pond, that we would like to investigate today. But if you and Carolyn want to ride up to Christiana and do some interviewing, then we could double our efforts. Frankly, John, it seems we are coming to the end of our options on the island. There are so many places to hide someone. She might not even be on the island still.

174

We have to face that possibility." The director of the search team was trying to be tactful as he pointed out the obvious possibilities involving prostitution rings.

"It's entirely possible that she has been taken to another island. There are so many in this part of the world."

"I can't just give up. She's my only child. My daughter and grandchild are depending on us."

"I know how hard this must be for you John. I have a daughter myself. That is part of the reason why I was so willing to put this team together. My heart goes out to you and Carolyn. I just don't know what more we can do at this point. We are running low on funds. It's been three weeks. If something were here, we would have found it by now. You know that."

Reluctantly John had to agree. It had been a frustrating and exhausting three weeks. He could see the exhaustion telling on Carolyn's face. He held her each night as she cried into his shoulder. They were reliving the horror of losing Elizabeth months before. But what was he to do? With all of his heart he believed his daughter was still alive. And Carolyn did too. Or were they just in deep denial about it all?

"I understand. Perhaps Carolyn and I can return home and begin fundraising. We appreciate all your help. We can't thank you enough. I'll talk to Carolyn tonight about making arrangements to fly home at the end of the week. I'm not sure she will agree."

"I will understand if you two can't give up the search just yet. I don't know that I would be able to either."

They shook hands as the director stood up to leave. They had been sitting on the verandah overlooking the pool and the beach while having coffee and breakfast. He had let Carolyn sleep in an extra hour. She had looked so weary the night before. It was probably a good thing that she didn't make this morning's meeting. She would be hard to convince that the search was rapidly approaching the end. It was going to break her heart. Still, there was no evidence, other than the tip from a tourist that his daughter had ever been on the island.

John looked out at the ocean. The azure waves were peacefully splashing ashore. He closed his eyes. The gentle sound of paradise soothed his troubled soul. He had never before been in such a beautiful place and felt such conflicting things in his spirit. The island was a place where people came to relax and enjoy themselves. It was a place where rich Americans came to get away from the rat race and the stress. Yet, a few miles up into the mountains, the islanders were struggling with poverty and deprivation. Few tourists ever saw that side of the island. They did not see the dirty barefoot children and their tiny homes playing beside the road with a skinny calf on a rope. They did not see the women struggling to cook a meal over an open fire with only a couple of dented pots and no running water. Every time John saw a little native girl, he saw blonde hair and blue eyes. He saw Elizabeth smiling back at him. Every time he saw a Jamaican infant, he longed to feel his grandchild in his arms.

Tears were rolling down his cheeks as he sat and thought about the lives these people lived, and how much he had in contrast. And how much he had lost. He had a choice; he could pick up the pieces and move on with his life, or he could stubbornly hold on to the bitterness of losing Beth and let it destroy him. If he never saw Elizabeth again, at least he had the blessing of raising a beautiful healthy daughter with every privilege imaginable afforded to her. God had truly blessed Johnathon Merriweather in this life. He could not be bitter at God, no matter how much his heart ached

177

for his daughter and unborn grandchild. God was still God. He would see them through this.

Guess I better go talk to Carolyn about going home. God, please help us through this. Please show us the way to peace through this trial. If my daughter is still alive, please help us find her. Show us the route to take to get her back. Protect her from evil. God, if something has happened to Elizabeth, if You have chosen to take her home to You, please help us gain some closure. Please help us find out what happened. Help us find her body or someone who knows what happened. God, we trust You to do what's best for us and Elizabeth. Help us accept your will. In Jesus' name, Amen.

179

Chapter 17

Hope Floats

Chris had attended church all his life, but had never chosen to accept Christ as his personal Savior. He had been taught all the Bible stories, learned all the children's songs, and had gone to Vacation Bible School every year. But now that he had accepted Christ, he had a burning desire to tell everyone he came in contact with about this grace that had been afforded him and changed his life. He was determined to make an impact in the life of his friends. He wanted to find a place where he could serve and show his love to the One who had lifted his burdens and made him clean.

"I'd like to work with the youth, Bro. Dave," he said that afternoon. "Is there anything I can do to help with the youth program?"

"Actually Chris, I'm so glad you asked. We have a new youth leader who would love to have an assistant. As a new Christian, I don't expect you to take a teaching role, but you can assist him with chaperoning and organizing his weekly meetings and activities. That way, you can get a feel for what we are all about. In time, you will pressed into greater service as you grow in your Christian walk. How about it?"

"Sounds great. When do I start?'

"Bro. Greg is in the process of planning the annual canoe trip to float the Buffalo. Does that sound like something you would be interested in?"

"Man, I'd love to. Thanks, Bro. Dave. I won't let you down."

By the time the day of the trip finally arrived, Chris had become an integral part of the leadership of the youth group. He had shared his heart with them in testimony one Wednesday night, and fifteen teenagers had responded to the altar call and gotten saved. Chris was beginning to realize that the trials and heartache he had suffered on his way to becoming a man had all been in preparation for this ministry. He embraced his calling with enthusiasm and eagerness.

As the bus crossed the Tennessee River at Parsons, a pang

181

of sadness filled Chris. This was where they had found Beth's backpack. He hadn't realized they would be taking this route. The memories of those winter months brought the bitter bile to his throat. He closed his eyes and willed the memories to stay in the recesses of his mind. He would not let the guilt that he felt over Beth's pregnancy and disappearance keep him from ministering to other kids. This was their day. Whatever pain he felt, he would try to overcome it, and make it a memorable event for them. Still, inside he felt the unmistakable presence of Beth pulling at his soul. *Could she still be alive out here somewhere? Beth, where are you?*

The hot summer sun beat down upon the group as they piled into their canoes at the put in point two at a time, the stronger of each pair loading in the back. Chris thought it would be wise to pair the teams in boy-girl fashion, with a strong male in each canoe. Chris's canoe went last, so he could bring up the rear and account for any strays. The youth leader was at the head of the party of twelve silver canoes gliding out into the rural countryside.

The young man that had unloaded the canoes offered Bro. Greg a tip as he boarded his canoe.

"If you keep to the left when you reach the fork, you will come across a good swimmin' hole about halfway into your trip. It's got a good beach for you to stop and eat your lunch-- that is, if you haven't lost it in the river." And then the man laughed, jumped in his truck, and hollered over his shoulder, "See you in a few hours at the pull out point."

The group sang choruses while paddling their way toward the pull out point. Every once in a while the current would swirl and eddy around a fallen tree, and if the canoers weren't careful, they were pulled toward the tree and tipped. The teens would pop up laughing as they pulled themselves back into their canoes and continued on their way. Chris could hear shrieks occasionally from the girls ahead as a snake would swim too close to the canoe.

"Just keep paddling," he would call out. "They're more afraid of you than you are them."

The scenery held the group spellbound as pristine waters unfolded before them. The sights and sounds of the city life faded to a million miles away. They stopped to admire the multi-layered limestone out-cropping. They waved as they passed the occasional camper or trail rider on the shore. And then, after a while, there were no more campers. There were no more signs of civilization.

It was earth and river and sky-- nature in its purest form, the miracle of God's creatures and creation. *God, you are so awesome. Thank you for this day. Thank you for loving me so much,* prayed Chris.

"I can't see the rest of the group anymore. We should catch up." Lindsey spoke, interrupting Chris's communion.

"Sorry. I just got caught up in it all. They're not far ahead."

Chris and Lindsey began to paddle a bit faster, and soon they rounded the curve. Before them lay a fork in the river.

"Which one should we take?" asked Lindsey.

"Hm. There's supposed to be a spot to swim somewhere up here. Can't remember if he said right or left. Doubt if it matters. They probably merge back into the same vein eventually. We might have to double back if it's the wrong one, though."

"Well, which do you think?"

"Right. Let's take the right one."

"You're the boss," she laughed, and they paddled on. Several minutes passed, but there was no sign of the rest of the group. The brush along the riverbanks was steadily growing denser and wilder.

"Must've been the other fork."

"Probably so," answered Chris. "Don't worry. They'll wait for us at the lunch spot."

"You two lost?" spoke a voice from the riverbank.

It startled Lindsey, who having gotten used to the solitude, jumped and nearly tipped the canoe. Chris noticed the word "catfish" spray painted in red letters across the side of the canoe. Otherwise, it was identical to the craft they were navigating. Catfish was sitting on his overturned canoe eating a fresh tomato. The juice was running down his chin and staining his yellowed t-shirt. He had been expecting Poke to meet him any minute and was slightly irritated that these greenhorns had missed the fork that took them away from his property.

"Well, I wouldn't say 'lost', exactly. I think we took the wrong fork."

"Lookin' for the swimmin' hole?"

"Yeah. We're supposed to stop there for lunch."

"Shoulda took a left." Catfish took another bite and stared at the girl in the front of the canoe.

"Purty day for a float down the Buffalo, ain't it."

"Couldn't have asked for better weather. What do you

suggest we do?"

"Yer closer to it by turnin' around and headin' back to the fork the way youn's came. Besides, it's pretty rough past this point."

"Okay. We'll do that. Thanks for your help mister." Once they had gotten out of Catfish's hearing range, they discussed the interchange.

"Well, that was so nice of him to help us out like that," Chris began.

"Yeah, but he sure scared me out of my wits. I about jumped ship."

"That was kinda funny. He was rough lookin', but nice."

"Can't judge a book by its cover," Lindsey replied as they finally reached the correct fork in the river and caught up to the group.

"Who was them younguns I passed?" Poke asked when he arrived moments later.

"Stupid tourists don't listen. Got one canoe in every bunch, I reckon."

Back at the trailer, Beth Merriweather was sitting under the shade tree and shelling a bushel of purple hull peas. Now and then

186

she would stop to wipe the sweat from her forehead with her elbow and wish for a gentle breeze to cool her weary frame. Catfish had warned her to be finished by the time he returned. Or else.

Chapter 18

Hope Flies

Beth shelled the last of the peas and ran her hands through them, tossing out any dried or rotten ones. She took the enamel dishpan into the trailer, washed them carefully with a jug of distilled water from the fridge, and put them into freezer bags. Her back ached from sitting on the straight-backed chair. She let out a heavy sigh and swatted at a fly flitting around her head. She longed for a long, hot shower. Catfish promised her the new house would have indoor plumbing, but had conceded in the meantime for her to bathe in the river now that the weather was warm. She had learned not only to look out for snakes, but to listen for the tell-tale rattle as well. She had learned so much about life and what it took to survive it, and these times along the riverbanks had become her solace. The cool river water felt great to her swollen feet. Catfish had gone to check the crops, but she knew that he watched her every move. She knew by now what a ruthless man he could be. Her fear of him made her irrational. Catfish was everywhere, knew everything, and could appear at a moment's notice to drag her back by the hair of her head.

The water was crisp and soothing, sparkling as the sun glinted off its surface. The daylilies along the riverbed had bloomed, and the banks were aflame in orange and red. Butterflies flitted from stalk to stalk as did honey bees gathering their precious nectar. If Beth had not known better, she would have sworn this was Eden. She stepped out further and felt her body being buoyed effortlessly by the water. It felt good to float, to feel free.

After swimming and cooling off a bit, she made her way to shore, grabbed the soap and headed back to waist deep water. Naked as the day she was born, Beth began to take inventory of her changing body as she slid the soap over it. Her breasts were heavy

189

and round. Her navel was protruding, and she had stretch marks on the sides of her belly. Her legs were unshaven, and her feet did not resemble her own. She barely recognized her own body. Her hands were stained a deep purple from the peas; her fingers were cracked, her palms calloused, and there was nothing left of her fingernails but jagged stumps. She rubbed her fingers together, furiously lathering, trying to lose the purple stain, but nothing she did could remove it, and so she gave up and lathered her hair.

She felt the baby kicking inside her as the cold water ran down her body. She wondered if it was a boy or girl. She wondered what she would name it. She imagined that she would at some point return home with the baby, but that was as far as her imagination took her. Thoughts of her mom standing in the door with a disapproving frown, thoughts of her father angrily shouting, thoughts of Chris acting like he didn't know her -- all these thoughts crowded into her mind at once. And she knew that leaving Perry County would only add to the heartache she had caused everyone. If only she had made a different choice that night. Would things have been different if she had actually made it to that clinic? Could she have faced her parents then?

If only she had known then what she knew now.

Beth leaned her head back into the water to rinse out the soap. The sky overhead was cloudy, as if it were trying to muster up a shower. Bath time was over. Just her luck, she thought. And then spoke aloud, "Why me, God? Why me?" But no answer came. She stood up in the water and cradled her swollen belly. At that moment, a delicate Luna moth came to rest on her navel. It batted its fragile wings for a few seconds as if pondering its next move. Beth caught her breath and smiled. Then it flitted softly up into the air and hovered over her as if to say in that quiet moment, "I am here, child. Look up, look up!"

PART TWO

Chapter 19

Between a Rock and a Hard Place

July 2005

The summer night song of crickets and frogs intermingled with the bellowing laughter coming from within the cabin. Sheriff Rus Wright eased the squad car to the edge of Hurricane Creek Road and cut the lights. He wanted no sirens or flashing lights tonight to warn the group of his arrival. He was acting on an anonymous tip that not only was illegal gambling going on inside the cabin, but the sale of illegal narcotics and marijuana.

The sheriff had an inkling that the information came from a disgruntled party that had lost a great sum of money in last week's game, but he couldn't prove this. The call came in over the TIPS line. The caller would not have to reveal his name. He would hate to have to bust these good old boys for gambling and possession, but this was an election year. A good haul would boost his standings in the race. He would hate it even more if he lost the election.

At the time that Sheriff Wright was voted into office nearly eight years ago, he was the youngest sheriff in the state. This distinction had drawn much criticism and doubt from his constituents. He had fought a hard battle to gain their trust, and he often felt as if he were proving himself to the public on a daily basis. Every arrest, every public appearance, every private appearance was under their watchful eyes. The last election had been closer than he cared to admit, yet he had overcome his opposition. He had put everything into this career. He would be careful to ensure that his integrity was in no way compromised tonight.

The sheriff wiped his brow with a white handkerchief as he made his way up the road toward the cabin. He was sweating profusely--not from being nervous, but from the overwhelming humidity. It was just after dark, and the digital read out in his car still read 93 degrees. It was mid-July, and there was not even a breeze stirring despite the forecast for rain overnight. The laughter wafted down to the road. There was a party going on inside, he was sure. But was there evidence of more corrupt behavior? He was about to find out. He raised his arm and waved the hanky to the deputies that had just arrived and parked behind him. There were five of them--all wearing pullover Polo shirts with Perry County Sheriff Department badges visible. They all were armed, but were under strict orders to hold their fire unless fired upon first. A loss of human life would surely hurt his chances of being re-elected. That was the last thing he wanted. He liked Old Poke and most of his fishing buddies. He halfway hoped there would be no drugs to find, and that he could just arrest them on the gambling charge.

If they found drugs, it would mean that there were others involved. Was it possible that the big drug cartels of Chicago and other places had finally reached the wilderness of Middle Tennessee? It was a sobering thought. He prayed the informant was wrong. Sheriff Wright had been in law enforcement all of his adult life. And although he was only in his late thirties now, his instincts were usually correct. The prickling up the back of his neck told him it was always better to err on the side of caution.

The search warrant provided a no-knock clause if there was danger present or a chance of losing valuable evidence, but Sheriff Wright had decided on a quick knock, announce, and enter approach. Two officers remained with the sheriff while the other two went to the back of the cabin. All had their weapons drawn and ready to fire if necessary.

"Sheriff's Department. Open up!" Sheriff Wright yelled after a quick knock. He immediately kicked in the door with his gun drawn.

"Everyone down. Now!"

The five men inside the cabin had no time to respond. The other officers had entered from the rear and were immediately on the scene. They had trained their weapons on the five horror stricken men cowering in fear with their hands in the air.

"No one move. I have a search warrant for this property, Poke."

"Search warrant? For what?"

"Boys, cuff the other men and take them outside. Be sure you read them their rights."

"Wait just a minute, now, Rus. We ain't doin' nothin' wrong here."

"Illegal Poker game going on tonight. And if my sources are correct, a little bit of drug dealing on the side."

"Drug dealing? What? We just good ol' boys out to have a lil fun..."

"Sorry, Poke. But we have to search. You're going to stay here in the house with us, so you can verify we aren't planting any evidence. And you better pray that none turns up. This is a serious offense. You know how I feel about drugs in my county. You know how Judge Fields feels about it."

Just then one of the deputies appeared with an empty baggy in his hand.

"Cocaine residue, boss."

"I see. Anything else?"

"Oh yeah. Found about 10 baggies of marijuana in the bathroom. Half of them emptied into the toilet, and few rocks of crack."

"Then my sources weren't just blowing smoke up my--"

"Boss, we found about fifteen thousand cash stashed in the

living room. Looks like an awful lot of money for a regular Poker game."

"Tag that as evidence too. Looks like we're going into town, Poke. You have the right to remain silent. Anything you say can and will be used against you in court. You have the right to an attorney. If you cannot afford one, one will be appointed to represent you before any questioning. You can decide at any time to exercise these rights and not answer any questions. Having these rights in mind, do you wish to talk to me?"

Poke hung his head in silence. His mind was racing. Who was the source? Probably old Vern. He was still sore over losing that seven hundred a couple of weeks back. Could have been Vern's wife. She was one of those Bible-toting fanatics like Inetha. His thoughts turned to Catfish. It was his fault they were all in this predicament. It was his fifteen thousand dollars stashed in the living room. Why had he ever let Catfish talk him into stashing the money here? And where was he anyway? Come to think of it, Poke had not seen Catfish in several days. He was probably running a load back down to Memphis. Well, he wasn't going to take the rap for this one. The gambling charge was plenty.

197

"Ain't none of that dope mine, Rus. The boys brought all that in."

"You think the judge and jury's gonna buy that, Poke? You're looking at hard time for dealing. This isn't a misdemeanor you're playing around with now. Maybe the powers that be would be willing to cut you a deal for less time if you were to come up with a few names, sources...producers."

"You want to get me killed? I ain't a snitch, Sheriff."

"Looks to me like you don't have much choice, now, do you?"

"Hey boss, look what I found back in the bedroom." The young officer was holding up two generic videotapes with handwritten titles. "Hot Teen Babes. Babes in the Woods. Looks like old Poke here is into child pornography too."

Sweat was rolling off Poke's brow profusely. His eyes widened in horror. You could be a drug dealer in prison. You could be a murderer. But child molesters, perceived or otherwise, were as good as dead in prison. He had never molested any young girls. He had fantasized about it. But he had never acted upon his urges. And now he was facing child pornography charges on top of gambling

198

and drug charges. Poke saw the rest of his life turning to vapor and fading like morning mist rising off the riverbanks.

"Now hold on. Hold on, jus' a minute. I can explain."

"Oh you have plenty of 'splainin' to do, Lucy. Let's get finished up here boys. It's going to be a long night at the station." He shook his head in disgust. It appeared that more than just the drug trade had managed to infiltrate the sleepy hills of Perry County. He wondered if even he could protect the county's children from the disgusting evil that had reared its ugly head tonight.

The three-car caravan made its way back into the town of Linden without incident. The town was quiet as they drove through except for a few teenagers gathered at the old Johnson Controls parking lot. The teens looked up at the three squad cars passing through. It was the entire fleet of Perry County, and it was highly unusual that they were all together. Usually at least one deputy was patrolling the nearby town of Lobelville which was also part of Perry County. There had to be something extraordinary taking place for all three to be out tonight. All three cars appeared to have passengers. As they passed under the street lamps, one of the teens recognized a face.

"Hey, ain't that Old Poke. Wonder what they got him for?"

"Aw probably just a bunch of old drunks got in a fist fight down at the chert pit. Happens from time to time. So my daddy says."

"Your daddy ought ta know...bet he was in there with 'em," one of the girls replied.

"Ha. Ha. That's so funny," the young boy said as he dropped his cigarette to the pavement and started to chase the girl across the lot.

Poke thought he recognized Pete's eldest boy in the crowd, but he wasn't sure. *I reckon there's gonna be hell to pay for all of us. Especially Catfish when I lay it all out for the sheriff. I ain't gonna spend the rest of my life in no cell at Turney Center...or worse. No way. If I'm going down, he's going down too. Can't help it if he does have a baby on the way. That was probably all wishful thinkin' anyhow. Inetha'd be better off without him.* He wiped the sweat from his eyes with his cuffed hands. *She got kinfolk over Tullahoma way that'll see about her. Crazy old cool oughta had more sense'n running drugs to start with. Now draggin' us off to prison with him. And they think they are gonna stick me with child pornography charges? Ain't no way...Yep, I'll make a deal with the devil himself if it'll get me out of*

200

this jam.

Chapter 20

Rattling the Chains

The fear that gripped Beth's heart kept her bound. Every time she tried to plan an escape her thoughts turned to poor Inetha lying in the field. Did Inetha die a slow, painful death? Visions of Inetha being butchered with the long knife that Catfish cleaned his nails with caused her to tremble violently at night. And even though Catfish had long since quit tying her to the bed, she was bound just the same as if the actual cords were there. Maybe Catfish had grown weary of untying her every hour during the night for her to go to the bathroom. Or maybe he had the crazy notion that Beth was actually growing fond of living here with him. She knew had no choice but to comply. She and her baby would die otherwise.

He had not acted upon his desires to consummate the relationship. Something had stopped him from putting his hands on her. Beth wondered if he had started feeling sorry for her. He had said that when the time came he would get Mama Lorraine to help with the birthing. He was worried that she might have trouble, being so young and small. But Mama Lorraine would know what to do. He had wondered aloud when the baby was due, but Beth had feigned ignorance about the time of conception. She had been with him six months now. If she had gotten pregnant in January, they would only have a couple more months, he said. September, maybe. Maybe late August. Hard to say. It was time they got the house in order.

"Liza. I'm a thinkin' it's 'bout time to get that other bedroom cleaned out, so little P.Jays will have somewheres to light. Don'tcha reckon?"

"P.Jays?"

"Phineas, Jr. Kinda like the name myself."

Beth closed her eyes and shuddered.

"He's been kicking an awful lot today. I think he's hot. Maybe it will cool off after the sun goes down here in a bit."

"Well, he better get used to it. Until I get the new house built anyways."

203

"New house?"

"Yep. Been savin' up to build me a regular box an' strip cabin. Won't that be something."

"You've been saving up? But you don't work."

"Shut your smart mouth, Liza. I got money. You forgettin' them crops out back? You forgettin' my little trip into the big city? I made plenty of them before you came along."

"How could I forget," Beth muttered dryly.

"I'm goin' out to check on them crops. They's just about ready for harvest. When I get back I want to see that bedroom cleaned out for Junior. I got big plans for that boy. Me 'n him's gonna spend our days a huntin' and fishin' and floatin' the Buffalo."

Before Beth had time to reply, the door slammed shut behind Catfish.

Left alone to her thoughts, Beth again felt a rush of panic. Her heart quickened. This was not the life she had intended for herself, much less the baby she carried and was soon to give birth to. Catfish had her life all mapped out for her. She would spend the rest of her days washing, gardening, and slaving for him and Junior. And what life would Junior have with Catfish as a father?

204

The baby kicked hard against her ribs as if rebelling against the very idea of it all. This sharp jolt awakened Beth's senses. At this moment there was no fear of what Catfish would do to her. At this moment, all that mattered was the well being of her child. Her maternal instincts were rising up in her. Their need for survival was beginning to supersede any fear that Catfish had instilled in her. She must find the courage to escape. If she allowed her baby to be born here in captivity, then Catfish would win. She would be under his rule forever.

"No, my sweet baby. You will not grow up in this dump. You will not be under his rule the rest of your life. I will find a way, my sweet. We will get out of here. Soon, I promise."

Beth waddled to the bathroom. She wasn't sure exactly how things were supposed to progress with the pregnancy. Health class had taught her the simple facts--nine months gestation, and then labor. They had even watched a video of a live birth. It was not something she looked forward to going through. Being seven months along, she knew that time was a precious commodity. Who was this Mama Lorraine, and where did she live? Perhaps she was not far. Maybe there were neighbors closer than she imagined.

205

Catfish's trailer could not be seen from the road, so Beth never saw the mailman. A couple of times the meter man's truck had pulled into the yard, and he had gotten out and checked the meter. Both times Catfish had been home and had threatened her with the knife if she made any noise from within the trailer. Other than that and the occasional visit from Poke, which always took place down by the river, no one had ventured onto the property in six months. She had naturally assumed there were no neighbors within walking distance, but maybe she was wrong. Maybe she could walk away from it all. Catfish had made her believe he would hunt her down and kill her in the most brutal of ways. And besides the fear of death, where would she go if she escaped. She could not go back home now with a child in tow and explain her absence. How could she explain her choice to have an abortion? How could she explain to her Daddy how she gotten in this predicament? She could not go home. But she could go somewhere. Anywhere would beat this miserable trailer and the dirty old taskmaster.

Once Beth had decided this, the rest was easy. Her actions were no longer the actions of a hesitant, fearful teenager, but that of a courageous mother tiger fighting for her unborn young. She had to act quickly. What would she need -- clothes, money, food? She ran to the closet in the bedroom she and Catfish shared. She flung open the door and began shoving boots and boxes out of the way. She was looking for a suitcase, an overnight bag, something to put a few things in. Something light enough to carry with her. It was already hard to walk, given the thirty pounds she had gained on her tiny frame. She rummaged through the items on the floor of the closet. It was getting late in the afternoon toward dusky dark, and the light in the room had grown dim. She stood up and reached for the cord to pull to turn the closet light on, and as it came on, above her head high on a shelf, a dark wooden box with gold trim caught her eye.

"I just wonder what that is," she said out loud. But she couldn't reach the shelf. She was too short. There was a straight back chair with a woven seat sitting against a far wall. Without the slightest hesitation, Beth threw the dirty clothes that were draped across it to the floor and drug it to the closet. She placed the chair against the wall to the left of the doorway and with a great effort, pulled herself up and into the chair. She was puffing when she stood up to reach for the box. *What if he comes back? Beth, you're*

207

crazy. He will kill you both.

Her hands were shaking as she reached for the smooth box and slid it off the shelf toward her. She held it firmly against her belly with one hand as she steadied herself against the doorframe with the other and made her way to the floor. She held her breath as she opened the wooden box, which resembled a t-shaped cross. She closed her eyes and sighed with relief as she saw what lay inside, a roll of bills, the keys to the truck, and five golden rings lying against the backdrop of a purple silk lining.

"Thank You, God," she spoke aloud. Now to find a bag for some clothing and food. She could take the truck. She couldn't believe her great fortune. There wasn't time to look for a suitcase. She wasn't even sure Catfish owned one. She went to the kitchen and got a plastic garbage bag. She threw a box of crackers into the sack and four cans of Vienna sausages. That would have to suffice. Back to the bedroom she raced as fast as her body would allow. She took the keys and the wad of bills and shoved them down into the deep pocket of her housedress. Then she wrapped the walnut box in another dress and placed it in the bottom of the sack. She could pawn the jewelry to survive. The last thing she grabbed was her North Side Indians shirt and jeans that she had long since outgrown, but they were hers-- the last vestiges that remained of who she once was. She put the chair back in its original spot and closed the closet door. She opened the blinds and peeked out toward the tree line. He had not returned yet. She had better take this chance. It might be her last.

She slid her feet into a pair of Mrs. Jones' old garden shoes and waddled into the living room. Her eye landed on the hilt of the hunting knife lying casually on the table beside the ratty recliner. Panic swept over her as she envisioned Catfish cutting her throat and throwing her in the river to die. She made her decision. The knife would no longer hold her prisoner. She could use it to defend herself. She grabbed the knife and shoved it down into the layers of the t-shirt that lay on top. She then made her way out of the hot, dirty trailer with the garbage bag slung over one shoulder and the truck keys in hand. Her heart was racing. Could she get to that truck and race away before Catfish returned?

Two steps, three steps, and then a quick run to the door of the GMC. She yanked it open, threw the bag inside, and pulled herself up into the driver's seat. She fumbled with the keys, but

209

finally was able to get them into the ignition. She pulled the driver's side door shut and turned the keys. The engine sputtered. It groaned. It ground. But it refused to come to life. She pumped the gas pedal hard and tried again. It sputtered, groaned, and ground.

Out of the corner of her eye, Beth saw a flash of movement running toward the truck. It was Catfish. He was running from around the corner of the trailer. His arm was raised. He brandished the gardening hoe like a bat. She pumped the gas. She turned the key. *Oh God, help me. Help me. He's going to kill me.* Beth locked the doors and kept trying to get the truck to start to no avail. Catfish swung at the windshield, cracking it all the way across. He was yelling obscenities at her.

"I'm gonna kill you. Get out of that truck! Get out of that truck now!"

By this time, Catfish had made it to the truck and was reaching for the door. Furious to find the driver's door locked he reared back with the gardening hoe and struck at the window. It did not break. He struck it again, this time finding success. He reached in to find the knob of the lock and pulled it up. Beth was

210

scrambling to the far side of the truck, desperate to unlock the passenger door, but the knob was missing. She fumbled with the garbage bag. She had to get to the knife. But the knife had shifted to the bottom of the bag. She could not find it. Catfish was still screaming and reaching for her legs to pull her feet first from the truck.

Beth's head was facing the floorboard as she fought to hold on and not let Catfish drag her from the truck. She knew she was a dead woman. With one hand she reached beneath the seat hunting a tire iron, a flash light, anything she could use to deter Catfish with. She felt something smooth and cold. She yanked it free. It was a brown quart-sized beer bottle. She was losing ground. Catfish was pulling her from the truck on the driver's side. She let go of the seat and allowed him to pull her toward him. As she passed the steering wheel and came as close as she dared to him, with all her might, praying to God for strength, she came up over her head with the beer bottle and smashed it to bits across the forehead of Catfish Jones, who much to his own surprise, slid to the ground and passed out. Beth looked down at the lifeless body and wondered if she had killed him. He wasn't moving, and his head was pouring blood from the cut the bottle had made.

Beth briefly caught her breath, and then reached behind her for the garbage bag. She grabbed it and slid out of the truck, stepping across Catfish and slamming the door behind her. She was a bit winded and dazed for a few seconds as she stood wondering what to do. A groan from behind her startled her to action. She must hide, lest he regain consciousness and come after her. The canoe! If she could make it to the river, she could set off in the canoe for civilization. Catfish would assume that she had taken off down the road, the logical route. She might just have a chance this way. But could she make it to the canoe? It was quite a way down the hill. She had to hurry to get out of his sight range before he regained consciousness. She topped the hill running, the white bag hitting against her leg. She felt the sharp point of the knife poking against her leg, but did not stop to see if it was actually cutting her. It did not matter at this point. She had to get to the canoe.

Once on the backside of the hill and out of sight of the trailer and truck, Beth stopped to catch her breath. She was holding her belly and gasping in deep ragged breaths. Her legs felt like they

212

were on fire, but she could not afford to stop for any length of time. A sharp pain grabbed at her lower belly. She thought it was just a muscle cramp from running so hard so fast. It never occurred to her that the baby was under great stress as well. It never occurred to her that this sharp pain might actually be early labor. That is, until the second pain struck, and then the third, a few yards on down toward the river. She could barely see the outline of the canoe, a small sliver against the sand in the distance downstream. And then another pain hit, and she knew. There was no doubt that the baby was coming now. Now, when she finally had a chance to escape.

Oh God, what am I going to do? Please don't come now. Don't come now. Wait, baby. Wait til I get us to some help. Ohhhh... ohh...OHHH! Beth felt a rush of water and blood flow out from her as her water broke. Bent double in pain, she made her way slowly to a grove of trees, holding her belly, the tears intermingling with the huge drops of sweat that had formed. If she could just get to the grove of trees, they at least might afford her a small amount of protection. She had to lie down. She felt the urge to push as the pains came. She felt the baby's head. There was no time to lose. Holding on to the

213

trunk of a nearby pine tree, she lowered herself to the ground. Beth

gritted her teeth as great waves of pain swept over her, coming

faster and faster with barely any time in between. Beth felt between

her legs. The baby's head was out; one more great push and it

would be fully birthed. Beth stifled a scream as she felt the baby

ripping and pushing his way out of her. And then it was over. He

was out. She pulled him to her belly, all wet and bloody, and then

he began to wail. Terrified, Beth tried to stifle his cries. She held

him to her breast. She rocked back and forth. Finally, she

unzipped the cotton housedress and placed him to her breast. The

baby had no trouble latching on and began to nurse.

Thank God. Thank you God. Oh he's perfect. Then she felt the

cord and another great urge to push again as the afterbirth was

expelled. Beth fumbled for the bag next to her. She dumped it out

with one hand, found the large knife, and willed herself to cut the

umbilical cord tying the baby to her body. When she had freed

him, she took the extra dress that she had brought along and

cleaned and dried him as best she could. Then wrapped him tightly

in the soft blue t-shirt. Exhausted from his traumatic birth, the

baby slept against her. She must get to the canoe. Catfish would be looking for her by now. He had probably heard the baby's cries.

She laid him, wrapped in the shirt, on the grass beside her. She

quickly gathered up the food, the box with the rings, and the jeans

and put it all back into the garbage bag. She left the knife out--just

in case she needed it. Catfish would not harm her baby. She would

fight to the death for this beautiful son to whom she had just given

birth.

Her legs trembled as she pulled herself up using the trunk

of the tree and stood. She put the bag over her wrist by its loops

and held onto the knife. She leaned against the tree on her elbow

and scooped the baby up with her free arm. She fought the

dizziness that was threatening to overtake her, gathered her

courage, and began the trek downstream to the canoe. The journey

seemed like forever, but only took Beth half an hour. She breathed

a silent thank you to the Lord as she finally reached the sandy shore

where the canoe lay. Exhausted, she managed to finally flip the

canoe over and place the bag inside on the bottom of the canoe.

Then she placed the baby on the bag, which was padded with the

jeans inside. It was the best she could offer this new little one, for

the time being. She promised to make it up to him somehow when

215

they had reached safety.

Blood was still running from the cuts the knife had made in her leg on Beth's run downhill. Her face was streaked with tears and sweat and blood and dirt. But she was alive. And her baby was alive. Determined to get them both to safety, she tugged with all her might on the canoe, moving it inch by gut-wrenching inch with her toward the murky green water. Beth's world was spinning. A kaleidoscope of trees, water, and sand began swirling around her. She shoved the boat out into the current, intending to step inside herself and pull away from shore, but the current pulled the canoe faster than she could respond. Beth grabbed for the canoe, and suddenly lost her balance. Her body was falling. She felt the cool water swirling around her legs as she fell half in and half out of the water, her head striking a huge red rock on the shore, and the kaleidoscope faded to black as the tiny newborn floated calmly away into the approaching night.

217

Chapter 21
All Hell Breaks Loose

Back at the jailhouse, the interrogation was growing quite heated. The sheriff had questioned Poke over and over about the source of the drugs and the child porn tapes. Poke had was resolute in his denial. None of the items were his.

"Ain't mine, Rus. The boys brought that stuff in."

"Do you really expect me to believe that? There was over fifteen thousand dollars there, Poke. You had to have been selling it. And I want to know where you got it. You got a crop stashed out in the hills somewhere?"

"No, I don't have no crop out nowhere."

"Just tell me where you got it. We can make a deal, Poke. You know you're facing prison time."

Poke was sweating buckets. He and Sheriff Wright were sitting at a small wooden table. There were no fancy two-way mirrors, only a lone camera filming the interview from high above. Poke fidgeted in his seat. Sheriff Wright took a pack of cigarettes from his pocket and offered one to Poke.

"Nah, I don't want that. I want out of here."

"What's the matter, Poke. Not your brand, eh? You prefer them funny left-handed cigarettes. Well, this is the best you're gonna get here."

"You think you're funny, don't you. Who told you about the weed? Vernon?"

"Now don't you worry about that none. All you boys will get your just desserts."

"Boss, the National Weather Service has just issued a Severe Thunderstorm Warning for Perry and Decatur counties with high winds and hail likely," interrupted Shorty the dispatcher.

"All right, Shorty. Looks like we're in for a little rain. Maybe it'll cool things off. Keep an eye on the radar. Me and Poke are gonna be here awhile longer."

"Sure thing, boss." And he closed the door behind him.

"Now back to matters at hand. Poke, are you prepared to sacrifice your freedom for whoever it is that you say is responsible for these drugs and tapes? These are federal charges, boy."

"Who you callin' boy, there. You better watch yoreself."

"I never would have figured you for a child molester, Poke. What else you keepin' hid?"

Poke jumped up from the chair prepared to rip the lawman's head off, but the door to the room swung open with no warning and the dispatcher ran in.

"Boss, a tornado has been spotted just across the river, moving at 90 mph. We're in the direct path of the storm. We've been advised to take cover immediately!"

"Goodness, Shorty. Ninety miles an hour! That's right on us! Come on Poke. Let's get you back in the cell."

They were just outside the room and headed down the narrow hall that led to the prisoner area when the lights flickered for a second and went off. They could hear the roar of the storm as it blew overhead.

"Get down Poke."

"We is gonna die. We is gonna die right here in jail. Oh

God, we is gonna die."

"Shut up Poke, and cover your head with your hands."

They got down in a squatting position against the wall and covered their heads. The wind was a fierce howling monster. They heard the sound of breaking glass. A loud clap of thunder caused Poke to shriek.

"Oh God, I don't wanna die. I'm guilty. I did it. I smoked that weed I got from Cat. Cat, forgive me buddy. I know you got a youngun on the way and all, but I can't take the rap for ya. I did watch them movies. I slept with Pete's wife, and I stole them fancy rims from Andy. I did it all that, God. I'm guilty. I don't wanna die," he wailed.

If the situation had not been so dangerous and so dire, the sheriff would have laughed at Poke's confession. He was crying and praying and admitting to every sin he ever committed. *Did he say Cat sold him the weed? I wouldn't have guessed that.*

Suddenly there came a great whooshing sound as part of the roof was torn back, and the rain suddenly was pouring in. A two by four roofing stud snapped in two, and asphalt shingles fell within inches of the two. Golf ball sized hail was falling around them and

221

on them. And then as suddenly as the storm hit, all went silent. The sheriff called out to the prisoners down the hall.

"Everyone okay in there?"

"Yeah, we're okay. Y'all?"

"We're fine. Just part of the roof gone. Come with me Poke. Let's get a flashlight."

They felt their way along the wall until they reached the door to the office where the dispatcher had hunkered down under a desk.

"Shorty, you alive in there?" the sheriff called out into the darkness.

"Yeah boss. I'm fine."

"Look in that top right drawer of my desk and get the flashlight, would ya."

In a few seconds the flashlight was turned on and trained to the ceiling.

"No damage in here. What about out there?"

"Lost part of the roof, but I believe the building is sound."

"Prisoners all accounted for?"

"Well, I think we liked to have lost old Poke to a heart attack, but other than that, yes."

The telephone interrupted their conversation, and Shorty took the flashlight and headed for the phone.

"I'll get the generator going, so we can get some power and get back up and running. If we sustained damage, then a whole lot of other folks did too. That's probably the first of a passel of calls." The sheriff led Poke back the cell, much to Poke's dismay, where Pete, who had heard his frantic confession was waiting with a not so happy expression. *Serves the old coot right,* thought the sheriff as he turned to go.

Shorty replaced the receiver, and it began to ring again almost immediately. He let it ring as he shouted to the sheriff.

"There's folks trapped in Cedaridge Apartments. A group of neighbors are heading up there with chainsaws. The elementary school sustained a lot of damage, and the high school is just a foundation now!"

"Do the best you can with the phones. Hopefully the Rescue Squad didn't get hit and is able to respond to calls of injury. I'm going out to assess the damage. Call Tommy and Danny and see if they got any damage. If they can, get them to load their four

223

wheelers up and be ready to go out into the county. There may be more people trapped and in need of assistance. If you need me radio me. Keep me updated."

"You got it. Be careful out there,Boss."

225

Chapter 22
Breaking Free

Cold rain was pelting Beth's bleeding forehead causing her

to turn her head from side to side as if trying to avoid the irritation.

Thunder boomed above her in the darkness. Startled, she jerked

and tried to push herself up with her hands, only to slip and slide in

the mud that surrounded the rocky area where she lay. She was

lying with her feet submerged in the shallow edge of the river, the

water lapping at her waist. She groaned as her body fought to gain

purchase in the muddy ground. *What's happening? Where am I? Oh*

God, my baby. Where's my baby? The memory of giving birth in the

grove of trees flashed before her, and in a desperate bid for her life,

she clawed her way out of the mud. Her hands reached for the

rocks above her head; her feet scrambled to find gravel on the

226

riverbed.

The trees nearby were bending nearly to the ground from the fierce winds howling through them. Beth tried to stand, but the wind forced her back to her knees. All was darkness. She waited for the next lightening flash to catch a glimpse of her surroundings and get her bearings. She looked towards the swelling river, but there was no sign of the canoe or the precious newborn she had placed inside. Dazed and confused, Beth held her head and screamed in miserable grief and frustration.

"Help me. Somebody please. Help me and my baby."

Her cries were lost as they mingled with the roar of the approaching tornado. Hail began to fall from the skies. Beth was being stoned with golf ball size hail. She scrambled toward a narrow area where the bank overhung the river. She could find shelter there until the river rose. She hoped the storm would pass soon, so that she could search for her baby. She no longer feared Catfish and his punishment. This was a far more dangerous fight for survival. She prayed that God would be merciful and save the life of her little baby boy. She prayed that somehow, some way, he would be protected from drowning in the raging river. She felt

227

along the bank until she found a group of large tree roots to hold on to, and there she huddled in the water, praying and hoping against all hope that the tree above her would not come crashing down upon her.

Back up on the other side of the hill, Catfish had already regained consciousness. He wiped the blood from his eyes and felt the wound on his head. Liza had packed a powerful wallop, whatever she had hit him with. He had underestimated her, that's for sure. His whole future would be destroyed if Liza made it to town. He was tightening the loose distributer cap on the truck when the first few drops of rain started coming down. He had started loosening the cap whenever the truck was going to sit parked for a while, for extra insurance against Liza taking off. He shuddered to think where he would be if Liza had gotten it started. He might already be sitting in jail. No, that would not happen. He was going after her. She could not have gone far in her condition and in the dark. Not knowing the area, she would probably stick to the paved road. It would be easy to find her and bring her back.

Catfish dropped the hood and slammed it shut. He opened the driver's side door and put the flashlight back underneath the seat. The keys were still in the ignition. The keys. She had found

the keys. That meant she had found his money. And the rings. He

cursed aloud. If Liza turned him in to the police and gave them the

rings, then not only was he facing prison for drugs, robbery, and

kidnapping, but he was facing the death penalty for the murder of

Frankie Carnel, not to mention Inetha. His troubles just kept piling

up.

Inetha was his biggest regret. His temper had proved to be

his undoing that time too. He just couldn't stand to be talked down

to, and Inetha had called him white trash. Those were the exact

words she had used when she found out about the marijuana patch

down in the woods.

"Phineas Jones, you ain't nothin' but poor white trash. You

sorry, good-for-nothing piece of white trash. How can you bring

damnation upon our household by peddling that devil's weed. I'll

not have it, Catfish. I won't! I'm packin' my bag and goin' back

home. And I have to tell you, it's my duty as a Christian woman to

stop in and tell the sheriff what you been up to. If you're smart,

and I doubt that you got much sense in that old head, but if you're

smart, you'll burn that acre of sin before you get in more trouble than just losing yore missus."

He hadn't meant to kill her. He just meant to shut her up. All that talk about damnation and jail. All that preaching and hollering. He just wanted her to shut up. By the time he took his hands from around her neck, Inetha lay lifeless on the floor of the trailer. He had tried to bring her back to no avail. Inetha, his bride, was gone. *Why couldn't she have just shut up and done as she was told? Why?* He had dressed her up in her Sunday best, combed her hair as pretty as he could, and buried her with her Bible in her hands, which he crossed over her lap just like he had seen them do up at McDonald's funeral home. She would rest peacefully on the backside of the hill facing the east so she could rise to meet Jesus in the rapture when He returned. She would be proud he remembered that. His eyes welled up with tears. *She was a pretty good woman to put up with me. And now it's too late. If they catch me, they'll bring Ola Sparky out of retirement, and I'll fry.*

Catfish cranked the truck and threw it in reverse. The rain was getting heavier as he pulled out onto the main road. He couldn't worry about a little bit of rain at this point. He had to find Liza before she found the police. *Crazy kid. Now why couldn't she just stay put?*

Chapter 23
Water's a Rising

Catfish had gotten about a half a mile down the gravel

road. He forced himself to slow down and search for signs of Liza

in the ditches and along the sides of the road. Rain was coming

down in blinding torrents and pouring in through the broken

window and soaking him. By this time he was actually torn

between his anger at her for leaving and his worry for the unborn

child. He had grown quite fond of Liza and had made big plans for

them as a family. The girl had no patience. If she had just waited a

few more months, he would have had the money to build their

home. It wouldn't be so bad. Well, he would find her. He would find her and convince her that it was in her best interest to stop this foolishness and come home before she hurt herself, or worse, little P.Jays.

The wind was beginning to gather speed. Hail began to fall and bounce off the hood of the truck.

'Holy Cow!"

And then, all at once, he heard the brutal pounding of it against the roof of the truck. It beat against the metal roof with such force that Catfish feared it would tear through the roof or break the windshield. Large stones of hail came through the broken driver's side window and hit him on the shoulder and face. Frantic to get out of their painful blows, he pulled the truck to the edge of the road and cut the engine. He scooted his body across the seat and managed to wedge himself down in the floorboard amid the garbage. He pulled a newspaper over his head and tried to stay dry as the storm pounded the truck unmercifully.

Then he heard it-- the loudest roar he had ever experienced. It sounded like a thousand freight trains rushing along in one breathtaking course, bent on destruction, bearing down on him and the old GMC. He felt the truck shake. He felt it suddenly begin to lift off the ground. He screamed out in utter terror.

"Ahhhhhhhh...uggghhhh..owwwww," he screamed as the truck was tossed into the air like a toy thrown from a toddler's hand. He was being thrown about in the interior of the truck. His head hit the dash, the door, the seat. There was nothing he could do to control the situation. He was at the mercy of the storm. And the storm was winning. After what seemed like an eternity, he felt the wind shift and the truck began to fall back to earth, rolling and tumbling as it fell.

The truck finally hit the ground with a jarring thud and rolled. He felt it rolling over and over. He was screaming out loud and begging God to help him, begging God to make it stop.

"God...Goddd! Make it stop. Make it stop!" he screamed breathlessly. "I swear I'll change. No more drug deals. I'll let her go. I promise. Make it stop!"

A huge clap of thunder nearly made him wet his pants. It split a nearby tree, the top of which came crashing down upon the already crumpled truck. In a few more seconds, the storm had abated and nothing was left but eerie silence and a rusted out GMC truck at the bottom of a deep gorge, soon to be filled with the

234

raging waters of the swollen Buffalo River.

Chapter 24

By Dawn's Early Light

Callie Mathis had just gotten up to start the coffee at dawn. She yawned and stretched as she poured her first cup. Her husband Sam yawned as he joined her.

"Did that storm last night wake you? It was a doozy."

"Didn't hear a thing."

"The electricity's been off, because the clock was flickering."

"Hm. Wonder if the river's up," she muttered as she made her way to the French doors that led to the patio. She pulled the curtains back. The sun was just coming up over the hill, promising a gorgeous summer day. Callie and Sam lived up on a hill that overlooked the Buffalo, but was well above the flood plain. Sam had brought Callie out to the property the day they became engaged and told her how romantic it would be to watch the sun coming up over the river every morning. So in the warmer months, Callie and Sam would have their morning coffee out on the deck and plan their day.

"Man, the river is way up," he remarked. "What's that? Looks like Flatwoods Canoe Rentals has lost one of their canoes. Maybe I better put my boots on and pull it to the house." There were a few limbs strewn about the yard, and the garbage cans had been overturned, but other than that, there were no other signs of the havoc that the storm had played in other parts of the county the night before. A strange sound filled the air, startling Sam into action. It couldn't be...but it was. The sound of a baby crying loudly pierced the foggy morning air.

"Is that --"

"Why, that's a baby crying. Where's it comin' from, Sam?"

Sam's face registered surprise and a puzzled fear. There wasn't a house for at least a mile. The baby's cries grew louder and more insistent. The cries were coming from the river. *My*

237

lands..there's a baby down there!

"Hurry. Bring me my pants and my boots. How in the world -- Hurry Callie!"

Sam jumped into his pants and boots and headed down the hill toward the river at full speed. The cries grew louder as he approached the canoe, which was half out of the water. Sam grabbed the canoe and pulled it completely onto shore. His eyes widened in shock as reached to scoop up the newborn from the bottom of the canoe. He looked up and down the river thinking that any minute a woman or man would appear to claim the child, but there was none in sight. His mind raced with the possibilities, but none of the scenarios he conjured up were logical, not to mention possible.

"Shhhh...it's okay now. You're safe now. Shhhhh." He held the baby against his chest and tried to soothe him, but the baby just kept crying. Sam reached inside the canoe and grabbed the plastic bag that the baby had been lying on. Maybe there was a note, a clue, something to tell him where the baby had come from. He would check the bag after he got the baby safely to the house. He never saw Catfish's name spray-painted down the side; he was just too excited. Callie would know what to do. She wasn't going to believe this.

Sam made his way back up the steep hill holding the baby snugly against him with one arm and holding the bag with the other. Callie raced down the deck steps to meet him.

"It *is* a baby! Sam, where did it come from?"

"Beats me. Craziest thing I've ever seen. Can't be more than a few hours old. Can't get him to stop crying."

"Let me have him."

Callie reached and took the baby from Sam's arms. She pulled the t-shirt away from the baby's body and noticed the umbilical cord still in place. The baby wailed from being exposed to the cold morning air. She quickly rewrapped the baby and took him inside. Sam followed behind her carrying the bag.

"I'm going to get a warm blanket. He's cold, and probably hungry. We need to get him to the hospital where they can check him out and give him some formula." She had handed the baby to Sam while she went in search of the blanket.

"Who would put a baby in a canoe and float it down the river? Just doesn't make sense."

239

"I know. Almost seems like a kid. A runaway, maybe?"

"But why the river? Why wouldn't they just leave him on our doorstep?"

"I don't know, honey. Get dressed. I'm going to call the Sheriff's office."

Sam picked up the phone to dial 9-1-1, but got no dial tone.

"The phone's out. Storm must've gotten water in the lines. Let's just get him to the hospital."

While Callie was getting dressed, Sam decided to check out the bag. The baby had finally gone to sleep, exhausted from his ordeal, so Sam tenderly laid him on the couch beside him. He reached inside the tattered bag and pulled out a pair of jeans. He threw them to the floor and reached again. This time he pulled out a tube of crackers and a can of sausages. *Food, but no formula for the baby. This baby's only a few hours old. Someone gave birth recently. Someone that was on the run.*

The last time he reached into the bag his hand struck something hard wrapped inside more clothing. He pulled the entire bundle out and unwrapped it revealing the gold trimmed walnut

240

box. He breathed a low whistle as he opened the box. There against the silk lining shone the five ancient treasures. He had no idea what he held in his hands, but he was sure that they were old and like nothing he had ever seen. *Someone stole these. The mother...she must have been on the run. She's stolen these.*

'You about ready? We really need to get to get him to the hospital," Sam asked.

"I'm ready. You drive. I'll hold the baby."

As the couple made their way toward town, they were amazed to see signs of the destruction the storm had left behind. At first it was just a few twigs and leaves scattered across the road, but a couple of miles farther down the road, they began to see trees with their tops sheared off, sheet metal twisted around their branches, buckets and odd items strewn across the fields.

"Looks like a tornado came through. I had no idea it got that bad."

"No wonder the phone's out."

"Look over there," Sam pointed to his left where a couple was out in their front yard cutting up a huge tree that had been uprooted. A mile farther down the road Callie exclaimed.

241

"Oh...Sam! Someone's been off the road. Look at the muddy tracks. Look at the ruts!"

"We're not the only ones with a story to tell, evidently. I hope they're all right."

When they finally pulled into Perry County Medical Center, the throng of patients in the Emergency Room overwhelmed them. An ambulance was parked by the entrance doors, and the paramedics were preparing to unload a patient. This much activity for the small town facility was rare. Something horrific had happened overnight. And Sam and Callie had slept through it without a thought.

"Excuse me, ma'am," Sam began as he approached the desk. " Ma'am, we have a newborn here that needs attention."

"A newborn? Where's the mother?"

"We don't know. It's quite a mystery. We found the baby floating in the river this morning in a canoe."

"What, you're kidding, right?"

"It's the truth with my hand up, miss. He appears to be okay, just hungry."

Sam and Callie did not notice the camera crew

242

closing in on them. WBBJ had been following the story since they had arrived in Linden soon after midnight. They had come to interview the hospital officials about the number of injuries that had been reported. Sensing a sensational story afoot, the reporter stuck his microphone in front of Sam's face and started firing questions. Sam was still holding the baby to his chest, trying to protect him from the media's onslaught.

"Excuse me, did you say you found a newborn in the river this morning?"

"Yes ma'am."

"In a canoe? How did all this come about?"

"Well, the missus and me, we drink out coffee out on the porch every morning and watch the sun come up. Had no idea a tornado had been through. Noticed the canoe down at the water's edge. That was when we heard Moses cryin'."

"Moses? His name is Moses?"

"Well, ma'am we don't know what his name is. We been callin' him Moses 'cause we drew him out of the river. Seemed fittin'."

"And you say he was in a canoe? Where do you think he

came from, sir? Were there any clues that might indicate who the baby belongs to?"

"He was lying in the bottom of a canoe wrapped up in a blue long-sleeved t-shirt. I have it here in this bag that was with him, along with some other things." Sam fumbled with the bag for a minute, then pulled the dirty shirt out and held it up. "Only thing I could tell was, it was probably a kid. Shirt's got an Indian chief logo on it with the initials, NSHS above it. Figured it was a high school mascot. The shirt was dirty and wet, so the wife wrapped the baby up in a proper blanket."

Just then the nurse came around from the counter and shooed away the press. She took the baby into her arms and disappeared through the double doors that led to the ER within.

The automatic entrance doors opened and a group of men ushered Catfish Jones in on a gurney. The reporter turned his attention to this new development, leaving Sam with instructions to wait there for a further in-depth interview. Sam and Callie craned their necks with great interest as they made their way to the lobby seating area. The media had completely surrounded the group of men.

"Stand back please. Not now. This man is in bad shape. Please," said the sheriff.

"Just a quick comment, if you will, tell us who this is and what's happened."

"I said, not now. I'll give you a press conference with full details later in the day. Right now we're still working on the rescue efforts. And this man needs treatment."

The paramedics pushed their way through the group and swept Catfish away to triage. The reporter shoved his microphone into the sheriff's face and continued.

"Have you been notified about the newborn that was just admitted that was found floating in the river?"

"Newborn? What? Um...no I haven't. As you can see, we've been quite busy."

"Mr. Sam Mathis and his wife, Callie brought the baby in a few moments ago. Mr. Mathis found the infant floating in a canoe at the river's edge in their back yard earlier this morning. No one knows how the baby got there and how the baby could have possibly survived the tornado. Any ideas on who this miracle baby they call "Moses" belongs to, Sheriff?"

245

"I will have to get back to you on that. In the meantime, I would ask that you please refrain from reporting until you get the complete set of facts."

The reporter did not answer the sheriff, but he promptly turned towards the camera and said,

"This is Hal Jacobs, for WBBJ-TV, reporting live from Perry County, Tennessee. Stay tuned in as we will be bringing you details from these stories as they become available."

247

Chapter 25
New Hope

In Jackson, John was sitting on the bed waiting for Carolyn to finish pressing his dress shirt. He had an important meeting this morning and wanted to impress his boss. He reached for the television remote and turned on CNN.

"Bad storm we had last night wasn't it," Carolyn said.

"Yep. But not near as bad as it got once it crossed the river. Usually those storms lose a little speed once they move out of our area. This one doubled in strength. They're calling it an F-4."

"Anyone hurt?"

"It hasn't said yet. Right now it's showing a lot of the damage. Perry County took a big hit. Lost several structures. The Middle School was flattened."

"Good thing it was at night. Can you imagine if it had hit

during the school day. F-4 is almost as bad as the one that hit us, isn't it?"

"Ours was an F-5, but you can bet there's plenty of damage."

John flipped the channels on over to his local station, Channel 7, WBBJ-TV. The reporter was interviewing a couple at Perry County Medical Center. Carolyn handed John the freshly pressed shirt, and he began to button it as he watched the screen.

"Excuse me, did you say you found a newborn in the river this morning?" the reporter asked; his voice was breathless and urgent.

"Yes ma'am."

"In a canoe? How did all this come about?"

"Well, the missus and me, we drink our coffee out on the porch every morning and watch the sun come up. Had no idea a tornado had been through. Noticed the canoe down at the water's edge. That was when we heard Moses cryin'."

"Imagine that," John said aloud.

"Shh. I want to hear the story," Carolyn answered.

"Moses? His name is Moses?"

249

"Well, ma'am we don't know what his name is. We been callin' him Moses 'cause we drew him outta the river. Seemed fittin'."

"And you say he was in a canoe? Where do you think he came from, sir? Were there any clues that might indicate who the baby belongs to?"

"He was lying in the bottom of a canoe wrapped up in a blue long-sleeved t-shirt. I have it here in this bag that was with him, along with some other things." John watched as Sam fumbled with the bag for a minute, then pulled the dirty shirt out and held it up. "Only thing I could tell was, it was probably a kid. Shirt's got an Indian chief logo on it with the initials, NSHS above it. Figured it was a high school mascot. The shirt was dirty and wet, so the wife wrapped the baby up in a proper blanket."

John stood to his feet. The realization hit him at the same moment it hit Carolyn. A blue long-sleeved t-shirt with NSHS on it.

"North Side High School!" They exclaimed in unison. And then turned back to the television, but a nurse had taken the baby and gone.

250

"Carol, could that have been Beth's shirt? Beth's baby...our grandbaby?" John's voice was excited and hesitant at the same time, as if she were too afraid to hope.

"She did have a shirt like that. I remember she liked to sleep in it because it was long. Come to think of it, I don't remember seeing it since she disappeared. Oh John, I know it's her! It has to be her!"

"Her backpack was pulled out of the Tennessee River at Perryville. That's on the border between Perry County and Decatur County. I'm calling the sheriff."

"Forget calling the sheriff. I have to see that baby. I will know if it's our grandson. I just need to see him. Get your shoes on, we're headed across the river." Carolyn's heart was in her throat. Where was Beth? How had her grandson ended up in a canoe on the Buffalo River? How did that tiny newborn survive the night in an F-4 tornado? *God, please let her be all right. Help us find her. Let my grandson be okay. Oh God, thank you. Thank you!*

Chapter 26

Free at Last

The muddy waters pulled and tugged at Beth's legs and

body. She clung desperately to the tree roots, and tried to remain

calm as the water steadily rose. She had to get out from the river

bottom. The wrath of the storm had dissipated, leaving in its wake

a wildly swollen river. Tree limbs and brush were sweeping by her

at a rapid pace. Several times Beth had to dodge to keep from

being knocked unconscious by a heavy log. She had tried to pull

herself along the edge of the bank and find a spot to climb out of the river, but once the tree roots ended, the bank was nothing more than silt and slime. She dared not turn loose, although her fingers had begun to grow numb.

There was a branch lying low across the river. Maybe she could, if she stretched really hard, reach the branch. It hardly looked sturdy enough to support her, but she knew she couldn't hold on much longer. The trauma of the birth and the lick on her head had sapped her of most of her strength. She was growing weary in her fight for survival. *What does it matter, my baby is gone now. I can't go back to Catfish. I'm as good as dead anyway. Maybe I should just let go, and let this be the end. My family thinks I'm dead anyway. I have nothing to live for now.* Beth was so tired. She was just so tired. Her grip was loosening. She felt herself sliding out into the current. She was letting go. Her last thought as her head went under was, *I'm going to be with my baby. I'm going to see God.*

The river swept Beth two miles downstream. She came up gasping for air, choking on river water, and then she came to an abrupt halt as her body slammed into a pile of brush that had collected against a fallen tree. Barely breathing, she lay there, half-conscious, across the pile of brush -- trapped by the tree with the

253

water rushing across her legs. The morning sun had appeared and was drying the water from her bruised and bloody face. Beth felt the warmth on her face. She saw light. She saw golden halos of light, transparent and celestial. And she felt love, so pure and transcendent that she realized that she must be nearing heaven's gates. There was no pain in her body. She was floating above the river and looking down.

Below her she saw the twisted form of a familiar girl. *That must be me. But if that's me, how did I get here. Wake up, Beth. Wake up.* Off in the distance she heard the sound of a thousand angelic voices. They were crying, "Holy, Holy, Holy" over and over in sweet tones of joyous praise. She wanted to get closer. She wanted to run to them, to hear their music, to sing with them. She wanted to see the face of God in all His glory. She wanted to see her baby. *This is heaven. This must be heaven. I never knew how wonderful it would be. Closer, I want to go closer. I want to go in.*

"Not just yet, my child," a Voice spoke. It was the most tender and loving voice Beth had ever heard. It sounded so familiar. So kind. "Not just yet, my beloved one. I still have work for you down there."

254

"But I want to see my baby boy. My baby...my boy..."

"You must go to him, child; he is not here. It is not your time."

"If he is not here, then where is he? How will I find him?"

"Love will lead you out of this barren land. Love will lead you to him. It is time for you to go my child. You are free."

Free. I'm finally free.

Chapter 27

Questions

As soon as the media cleared out, Sam made his way over to the sheriff, who had been standing at the ER admitting desk talking to the clerk about the night's events. Sheriff Wright wanted to wait around to make sure Catfish was going to pull through. He also had some reports to fill out, and he wanted to check on the ladies that had been trapped in the apartment complex. *Was that really only last night? It seems like light years ago. Man, I'm beat. And now there's this baby to investigate.*

'Um, Sheriff. I know you're kinda busy right now, but I wanted to talk to you about the baby we found this morning."

"I was just fixin' to ask you some questions about that. I hear your morning has been as strange as my night."

"Well, it certainly hasn't been your usual Friday morning, I'll grant ya that."

"Get Callie and let's go back in this little office here and get me up to speed."

"Come on Callie," Sam called. "Sheriff wants to ask us about the baby."

Callie rose to her feet and followed the two gentlemen to an office off the side of the admitting desk. In her hand she carried her shoulder bag and the tattered garbage bag. She felt a bit self-conscious about her looks. She had hastily thrown on an old jogging suit and ran her fingers through her hair. There wasn't time for makeup or even to brush her teeth. But judging by the looks of things, Sheriff Russell had had a bad night too. She doubted if anyone would notice or care what she looked like at this point.

The sheriff pulled up a rolling office chair as Callie and Sam sat in the two visitor chairs opposite the desk. He had so many

257

questions running through his mind. It was hard to concentrate as tired as he was. The events of the night before were telling on his face. He sighed, ran his fingers through his hair, and then rubbed his eyes before pulling a pen and a small notepad from his shirt pocket.

"Now where exactly did you find this baby this mornin' Sam. Was it you, or Mrs. Callie here, that found him?"

"Well, we both heard him about the same time. Callie and me were headin' out to the back deck to have our morning coffee. We noticed the river was up, and I spotted a stray canoe down at the edge of the water. When we heard that baby cryin' I grabbed my pants and shoes and took off down the hill."

"And what time was that this morning?"

"It was, oh I'd say about sun up."

"And what did you find when you got down to the river?"

"I pulled the canoe up on shore, and down in the bottom of the boat, lay this little fella, no bigger than a turnip. He was squalling his head off. He was laying on top of this bag here. Show him Callie what was in the bag."

Callie lifted the bag from off the floor and rummaged

around in the top of it.

"Well, the baby was wrapped in this t-shirt. But it was all soggy and dirty, so I cleaned the baby up a little and wrapped him in the afghan off the sofa." She handed the shirt over to the sheriff. He spread it out before him and inspected it. "NSHS. North Side Indians?" "It looks to me like some kid is in trouble. But the river? I can't figure out why they would put the baby in the river. What else is in that sack, Mrs. Callie?"

Callie handed over the garbage bag, and Sheriff Russell began pulling out the items one by one.

"Food. More clothing. Wait. What's this?" His hand was on the walnut box. He pulled it carefully from the bag. It was an odd size, delicately carved and gold trimmed -- not what he had expected to find. He ran a finger around the lid. He read the inscription. It still did not dawn on him that this was part of the stolen King Tut exhibit. The sheriff opened the lid. He wasn't sure what he had expected to find; he'd seen some crazy things in his job as an officer of the law. He caught his breath as the golden rings shone up at him from the dark interior. *Rings. Heavy gola rings. Stolen, no doubt. No money. No credit cards. No ID. A runaway. Wait.*

259

The runaway from Madison County. It all fit. But where was the girl? And what did the rings have to do with anything? She needed money to survive. She was probably going to pawn them when she got where she was going. Had she been living in the woods all this time? Breaking into homes for food and money?

"Thank you for bringing the baby and these things in. They will help us find the mother."

"But what will happen to the baby?" Callie asked.

"Right now, he will be placed in the custody of the Department of Human Services. All that will have to be worked out. I imagine he will become a ward of the State. Looks like his mother will be facing jail time when we find her for endangering the baby, not to mention theft charges. She's in a lot of trouble. Now, if you'll excuse me, I have a call to make. Thanks again."

Callie and Sam were at a loss as to what to do. They didn't want to leave the baby alone at the hospital. But what could they do but wait and see if the mother were found. Perhaps the girl's family could be located. Already they had fallen in love with the miracle baby they had named Moses. Callie was softly crying as she left the office.

Russell picked up the phone and dialed information. He wanted to call the Madison County Sheriff's Office to confirm his suspicions. If this baby belonged to the Jackson runaway, Sheriff Dameron would be involved. And he would have all the information on the case.

"Jackson, Tennessee. Madison County Sheriff's Department." Russell jotted down the number, dialed it, and then waited for an answer.

"Uh yes... this is Sheriff Rus Wright over in Perry County. I need to speak to Sheriff Dameron if he's in please."

"One moment, please."

"Sheriff Dameron speaking."

"Hello. Sheriff Wright, over in Perry County. How ya doin' this morning?"

"Well, better than you guys, obviously. What can we do to help you this morning, Rus?"

"Well, I've got this situation that's come up...in the middle of everything else. I think I have a lead on that runaway from Jackson back in the winter. What was her name?"

"Elizabeth Morgan. What ya got?"

"A baby's what I got. Couple brought it in to the hospital this morning. Found it floating in a canoe in the Buffalo River this morning after the storm."

"What makes you think it's connected to our case?"

"Listen to this. The baby was wrapped in a blue long-sleeved t-shirt with an Indian logo on it, and the initials NHS."

"Holy cow. She's still alive. Where is she?"

"Well, that's the thing. The mother was nowhere in sight. The baby was lying on a garbage bag that had some food and clothes in it. There was also some stolen jewelry in the bag--fancy stuff. Gold rings in a fancy jewelry box. She must be breaking in houses to survive."

"We've had our share of robberies and home invasions down here lately too. Is it possible she stole the stuff before she ran away? Can you describe the jewelry so I'll have a description."

"Well, it's not like anything around here. They are big and heavy. Feel solid. They have these almost hieroglyphic-looking markings on them. And they're in a walnut case with a purple silk lining."

"Purple silk...what the ...Son, I think you might have just

found the Tut Treasure."

"The what?"

"You remember, the King Tut exhibit was robbed back in January. Jewels never turned up. TBI's been working on the case for seven months with no leads. This is big!"

"But how would a seventeen year old pregnant runaway manage to steal them? Doesn't add up."

"I'm gonna put in a call to the TBI. Don't let those out of your sight." A nurse stuck her head in the door about that time and whispered,

"Mr. Jones has regained consciousness. The doctor says you have ten minutes."

"I think you better get up here so we can sort through all this and find the girl."

"I think you're right. Sit tight. Try not to leak it to the press. You know how they are."

"How well do I know. I 've got a press conference coming up this afternoon about the storm. Looks like we may have an even bigger story by then. See ya when you get here." After he hung up the phone, he nodded to the nurse.

263

"Thanks nurse. I won't be but a minute. I need to get a few details." Then his eyes widened as he remembered Inetha.

"We haven't even told Inetha yet. She must be worried sick. Poke said he didn't show up for the Poker game. 'Come to think of it, I don't even know if Inetha's okay. That little trailer may be demolished. I better get up there and talk to him, and then head on out to his place and check things out. I'll bring Inetha back in to town with me."

"Very good. I'm sure she will be relieved that he's okay. Doctor thinks he'll recover. Broke his ribs and his right leg, concussion, lacerations...lucky to be alive. Follow me. I'll take you to him."

'Um. Do you have somewhere I can lock this evidence up? Just 'til after I question Mr. Jones?"

"We have a medicine cabinet where we lock up controlled medications. No one has a key but me. I'm the charge nurse. Come with me."

265

Chapter 28

More Questions

After the sheriff had secured the evidence, he followed the nurse

to Catfish's room and closed the door behind him. Bruised and

battered, Catfish lay resting with his head elevated. He had a long

cut above his right eye, and his leg was in a cast. The sheriff could

not see under the hospital gown, but he suspected he was taped up

pretty good around his ribs as well. Catfish grimaced every time he

took a breath.

"Well, Cat, you look pretty rough. But I guess it could be

worse."

Catfish rolled his eyes and turned his head to the

wall.

"Yeah. I guess so."

"You remember what happened to you?"

"Remember? If I live to be a hunnert, I don't think I'll ever forget."

"It was an F-4 tornado. We've got a lot of damage across town. What were you doing out in the storm?"

Catfish couldn't tell him that he was out chasing down Liza. He couldn't tell the sheriff that Liza had hit him over the head with an empty beer bottle trying to escape.

"I was on my way to play Poker over at Poke's with the boys."

"I see. A little late weren't you?"

"I reckon that's none of your concern."

"Well, now. I suppose it is. See, Poke and the boys rode out the storm in the jail. They got themselves arrested right before the storm hit."

"Arrested. Aw, Sheriff you been knowing about them Poker games for years."

"Knew about the Poker. Didn't know about the drugs. Or the kiddie porn, for that matter."

"Kiddie porn?"

"Mr. Jones, I'm gonna have to ask you about your

267

involvement with Poke. Poke's in serious trouble -- facing Federal charges."

"Don't know nothin' bout no drugs or porn."

"Word has it you have a few crops out in the woods, Mr. Jones."

"Cut the Mr. Jones crap. You been knowin' me all yore life. Now you wanna turn on me in my hour o' need."

"I'd like to help you out, Cat. But I have to know about the pot. Poke says he was holding the cash and drugs for you."

The curtain was pulled back as a nurse in bright pink scrubs stuck her head in.

"Sheriff, Mr. Mathis is on the phone. Says he needs to tell you something real important."

"Mr. Mathis?"

"The couple that just left a little while ago."

"Oh...right. Don't go anywhere Catfish. I'll be back to finish this conversation."

The sheriff made his way to the nurse's station. Maybe Mr. Mathis had remembered an important detail about the baby.

"Sheriff Wright here."

"Sheriff. This is Sam Mathis, the one who found the baby."

268

"Yes sir. You remember something else?"

"No, but when I got home and loaded the canoe on the truck, I found a clue. Might help you out."

"What's that?"

"Well, it's got 'Catfish' spray painted in red down one side. I first thought it was one of Flatwoods Canoe Rentals'. Looks just like theirs."

"Hm. That's interesting. Thanks for calling back. That helps a lot. If you remember anything else or find out anything else, give me a call."

"Sure thing. How's the baby doing? The Missus is worried about him."

"I haven't heard, Sam. But I'll check on him for you. I'm sure these nurses are taking real good care of him."

"I surely hope so. Thank ya, Sheriff."

Sheriff Wright placed the phone back on the cradle and hurried back to Catfish's room. Catfish was struggling to get his shirt back on. He was sitting up on the side of the bed, his face red and grimacing.

"Now you just hold on there! You're in no condition to be

leaving just yet. The doctor hasn't released ya."

"I gotta get home and see if there's anything left of it."

"Don't you worry about that, Cat. I'm going out there myself to check on Inetha and tell her where you're at. Surprised she hasn't come lookin' for ya already."

Catfish's eyes widened, and his face went pale.

"Inetha...well, uh...the thing is...see...I haven't told anyone, but Inetha's gone. Left me for the Combine Insurance man."

"Left you?" The sheriff was becoming increasingly alarmed. *How does Catfish's canoe fit into all this? Was the girl hiding out near the river? And where was Inetha?*

"Catfish. Your canoe ended up three miles downriver this morning."

"Well I'll be -- that was some storm wasn't it."

"There was a baby inside it." The sheriff stated flatly. "Know anything about a baby and a missing girl?"

Catfish's eyes narrowed. So she had had the baby. He hadn't thought of the canoe. He had naturally assumed that Liza had left by way of the main road. He wondered how she had found the canoe.

270

"A baby! In my canoe? Did you get hit in the head last night, Sheriff?"

"I'm dead serious, Cat. We think the young girl is one that has been missing since January. She's a runaway. If you know anything about her, you better speak up now. You're in enough trouble with that farming you been a doing."

"I don't know nothin' about nothin'."

" Catfish, that baby needs its mama. Now are you gonna tell me what you know, or am I gonna have to arrest you?"

"Arrest me for what? You don't have anything to hold me on."

"Maybe I don't. But I got enough for a search warrant. I've got Poke who's going to testify against you. I got what he says is your fifteen thousand dollars in cash. If I find marijuana planted on your property, I don't reckon you'll be a needin' that."

The mention of his money brought Catfish around. Poke had no right to turn him in after all he'd done for him. Things sure had gotten messed up in a hurry.

"Now hold on, Sheriff. Hold on."

"I think you better get to talkin' Catfish. And fast."

271

"I want a lawyer."

"You'll get your lawyer. And your day in court. Tell me about the girl, Cat. Where's the girl? We need to find her."

"Stupid kid. Shoulda stayed put, instead a runnin' off during a storm with my --"

"With your baby? You don't expect me to believe that do you, Cat. Inetha wouldn't stand for that. Is that why she left you? You took the girl in? Where is she?" he shouted.

"I...uh.. I don't know. I don't know where she is. She took off last night. I was out lookin' for her when the storm hit. She must've had the baby last night. I expect if you found the baby in the canoe, she's probably drowned -- or she's layin' out in the woods somewheres. Lord knows she's been enough trouble to me."

"Well, you're not going anywhere in your condition. I suggest you use the time to get your facts in order." And as he turned to go, he paused. "And I promise you, Cat, if you've held that girl against her will, or harmed her in any way, there will be a price to pay. I better find that gal alive and well."

Catfish didn't answer. He was thinking about his choices

and what they had cost them so far. If he hadn't ever agreed grow the pot, he wouldn't have been in Memphis. He would never have run into Liza. Inetha would still be alive. He wouldn't be lying in this bed and facing jail time. He was in enough trouble without them finding out about Frankie and the rings. The rings! Liza would have the rings. When they found her, she would tell them where she got the rings. If she were still alive. At this point, he could only hope that she had drowned in the storm and taken those cursed rings with her. What did it matter now anyway? His hopes and dreams of having a family and home were all crushed. He was a broken man. There was nothing to do now but lie here and while away the hours playing this sad solitary game of what if.

Chapter 29
Glad Reunion Day

"Sheriff, there's a couple here that wants to see the baby. They claim it may be their grandchild."

The nurse had met the Sheriff in the hallway. Her voice was animated as she recounted how the Merriweathers had come rushing up to the ER desk demanding to see Baby Moses.

"They're in the consult room. I told them they would need to speak to you first, but they are adamant about seeing the baby. They're the parents of Elizabeth Morgan, the teenage girl that disappeared last winter."

"How did they know about the baby?"

"Saw it on the early morning news. Remember the reporters."

"I asked them to hold off on broadcasting til we got more facts."

"Evidently they aired the story, and the Merriweathers came on down."

"I suspect that this may be their grandbaby, but without finding the mother or doing DNA testing, we just won't know that. Okay, hang tight. And don't let anyone near the baby without my say-so. Not reporters. Not anyone."

"Yes sir. I understand."

The nurse headed off to instruct the staff about the baby as Sheriff Wright stepped inside the conference room. Carolyn jumped out of her chair to meet him.

"Where is she? Where's our daughter? Can I see the baby? What have you found out?"

"whoa...Hold on ma'am. Let's just have a seat. I'll tell you what I know."

"I'm sorry. We saw it on the news and hurried over. We're

275

certain that's our grandchild."

"What makes you so certain, ma'am?"

"The baby was found wrapped in a blue North Side t-shirt just like my daughter's. It has to be her. Where could she be?"

"Mrs. Merriweather. I've contacted the sheriff over in your county, and he is on his way over here. Should be here any time now, as a matter of fact. He's inclined to agree with you. He's bringing the case file. There's uh.. there's something else...in the bag that was found with the baby..."

"What is it?" John asked.

"There was food and more clothing and a box with stolen jewelry inside."

"Stolen jewelry?" gasped Carolyn.

"We think she was on the run and was breaking into homes and stealing to survive..." A sudden thought stopped the sheriff in his tracks. Sheriff Dameron thought these might be the Tut treasures. How would Elizabeth have come across them... unless...they were already stolen and stashed somewhere she was staying. But Catfish wasn't sophisticated enough to pull off a robbery of that magnitude. Was he?

"Sheriff? What is it?" John interrupted his thoughts.

"Um...Mr. Merriweather. I have a lead on your daughter's whereabouts, but I have to check it out. We don't know if this baby is your grandchild without finding the girl or doing DNA testing, which would take a few weeks. I'm going to check out this lead as soon as Sheriff Dameron gets here."

"Please, sheriff. Please let me see the baby. Just let me look at him, see if he resembles my Beth."

"I'm not sure that's a good idea. I mean, what if he's not."

"Then what would it hurt? The baby is okay, isn't he?"

"The baby is going to be fine. I'll okay it with the nurse."

"Look Sheriff, if our daughter is in the nearby area, she could be hurt. She could be trapped from the storm. Take me to where the baby was found. Please."

"The baby was found three miles from the home of the canoe's owner."

"What! You know who the canoe belongs to? What are we waiting for? Let's go now!"

Mr. Merriweather was shouting at the sheriff. It had been such a long night for the sheriff. The events of the last few hours were taking their toll on him. His patience was wearing thin. He just didn't have the energy to fight with the distraught father. And Mr. Merriweather was right. Elizabeth could be in grave danger, if she was still alive.

"Mr. Merriweather, you realize that we might not find her ... alive..."

"For heaven's sake, man. I've been wondering for months what happened to my daughter. I have to know one way or another. Now let's go! Carolyn, stay here, and take care of the baby. I'm bringing her back to you, I promise honey."

The sheriff picked up a phone on the wall by the door and rang the nurse's desk.

"Nurse, please come escort Mrs. Merriweather to the nursery, and let her see the baby that was brought in. She is not to take the baby from the nursery, and this is to be done with the utmost discretion. You understand? When Sheriff Dameron from the Madison County Sheriff's Department arrives have him escort Mrs. Merriweather to the conference room and wait for us. I'll check back in as soon as possible."

Sheriff Wright hung up the phone and turned to the couple.

"Thank you, Sheriff. Thank you!"

"Don't thank me quite yet. Let's go look for your daughter."

Chapter 30
I am Weak, but He is Strong

The next time Beth awoke, the river had gone back into its banks, and she found herself lying on the fallen tree and the pile of brush upon the muddy bank. She stirred slowly. *I'm alive! I'm alive!* Her head was pounding; her limbs felt like she had gone sixteen rounds with George Forman. Beth's hand went to her face, which was swollen and burning in the July sun. *How long have I been here? Wonder what time it is? Got to get help. But where am I?*

Beth looked up and down the river. As far as her eye could see, there was no sign of human life along the riverbed. She wondered how far downriver she had floated. She coughed and tried to move. Finally, she managed to roll herself off the tree and onto the sand and mud. Gradually she crawled on her hands and knees over to the embankment, which was higher up. She managed to stand, but felt the world spin as she did. The river had swept her

280

shoes away, and she was barefoot in the mud. Instinct brought her hand to her belly, and instantly the memory of the night's horror flooded over her. *The canoe. The baby. He was probably dead, drowned in the flooded river. My baby, my poor baby. But no...that Voice that had spoken to her. What was it the Voice had said? He is not here. You must go to him. If only I knew where to go. God, where is he? God help me...help me please. God I'm so tired. I can't go on. God, if you really, really love me, please help me get out of here. Help me find him. He needs me.*

The only thing Beth knew to do was to try to walk for help. She carefully made her way up the edge of the bank to dry land and surveyed her options. Which way should she go? She wasn't up to tackling the steep hill directly ahead of her. Maybe she should just follow the river. Surely it would lead to a road eventually. She wanted to go the opposite direction from Catfish, in case he was still looking for her. She was disoriented. Which way was the trailer? She thought she was going away from it, but she couldn't be sure. *Just put one foot in front of the other. Just keep walking. Keep going. You have to find help for your baby.* Every step she made felt like it would be her last. She trudged through waist high grass for what seemed like eternity.

281

Memories of before and after kept coming to mind. Her life was now defined by two things: before she got pregnant, and life after she got pregnant. It all came down to that first choice. Why had she decided to give in to Chris? One wrong choice had led to this unending misery. No, two wrong choices. She had chosen to abort the baby, or she never would have been in Memphis. She never would have run into Catfish. She wouldn't be fighting for her life now. She couldn't help but wonder bitterly what life would be like had she made a different choice that night -- the right choice. It could not have been any worse than what she was now facing.

Finally she made it to a clearing. She was sweating profusely, and her vision began to blur. *I can't God. I can't go on. I can't take it anymore.* And then her toe struck an outcropping of rock she hadn't seen. She stumbled and was unable to regain her balance. The green grass swirled with the blue sky. She rolled onto her back and stared up at the heavens. A large buzzard was circling overhead. *She let out a weak sarcastic laugh. So this is it. This is how it will end. I thought I had plenty of time.* Then all went black.

282

283

Chapter 31

Yes, Jesus Loves Me

"So, where are we headed?" John asked anxiously.

"We're headed out to the area where the baby was found. There was a name on the canoe. Catfish. Catfish Jones lives in this area. We hauled him and his truck out of the riverbed last night. He says Beth ran off before the storm, and he went after her in the truck."

"What! You talked to the man who has my daughter! Why didn't you tell us?"

"Because he is at the hospital in bad shape. I didn't want you trying to get to him."

"Get to him -- I'll kill him!"

"That was my thinking."

"What did he say? Has she been with him all this time? How did she get out here?"

"We didn't get that far in the questioning. The

284

minute I realized that Beth had been out in the storm in the canoe with the baby, and was probably still out there; I knew there was no time to lose. That's when you and Mrs. Merriweather arrived. There'll be plenty of time to question him after we find her."

"My little girl. In a canoe. In an F-4 tornado... She didn't have a chance, did she?"

"You're forgetting the baby survived the storm. That's one miracle. You got enough faith for another one?"

John closed his eyes and let out a deep breath. His eyes filled with tears.

"Beth is our only child. It hurt so bad when she disappeared. I had almost given up hope of ever seeing her again alive. Now God has brought me to her. She has to be alive...she has to be."

Sheriff Wright pulled up the long drive that led to Catfish and Inetha's trailer. The devastation that met them left them speechless. The spot where the trailer had set was now a dark, muddy, grassless patch of land. Several yards away lay the wreckage, barely recognizable. Insulation and metal and wooden beams were twisted in an awful, unnatural configuration. Underpinning was scattered about the yard, along with odd items

285

including the box springs from the bed. The ground was littered with debris; some of it hanging from nearby trees. A pitiful, skinny dog lay dead to one side.

"Well, so much for searching the trailer for clues," said Rus. "No sign of his wife either."

"You mean he had a wife?" John asked incredulously. "No one could have survived that." John stated flatly.

"We'll check the wreckage, but Catfish said she had taken off before the storm."

"Bethhhh," John yelled. "Beth!"

"He thought she had taken off walking down the main road, but somewhere between the trailer and the river, she had to have given birth. The baby wasn't over a day old. Still had the umbilical stump. Let's check the woods and then on down by the river. The rest of the search crew will be here shortly. The deputies and rescue squad all went home to see about their damage. Shorty was having to round them up."

The two took off in opposite directions with John yelling out Beth's name every few seconds. They spread out through the woods, several yards apart. Sheriff Wright drew in a sharp breath

286

when he came upon the marijuana crop. He whistled a low whistle. *He was doing more than just growing it for himself and a few Poker buddies. There's fifty thousand dollars' worth here.* The sheriff scratched his head. He was willing to bet that there was a larger cartel paying Catfish big money to produce. This was big. Perry County would be all over the news this week. But for all the wrong reasons.

"You found any clues?" he yelled over to John.

"Nothing. I'm heading on down towards the river."

"Wait for me." But John was already running off down the hill. He had to find Beth. A sense of urgency was bearing down in him.

"GO NOW!" the Voice said. "She's down past the river bend. HURRY!"

John was running blindly now, screaming her name as loud as he could. Running through the tall grass, running, nearly tumbling over his own feet.

"BETHHHHH! Beth! Where are you?" he called.

From the dark recesses of her mind, Beth thought she heard her dad calling her name. She tried to open her eyes. She tried to move. *I'm here, Daddy. I'm over here. Wake up, Beth. You're dreaming. WAKE UP!*

'Beth! Are you out here? Beth!"

Finally she managed to get her eyes open. She was still lying on the ground. The buzzard was gone. She hadn't imagined the voice. It was coming closer. It was daddy; it was! She opened her mouth and tried to yell, but her mouth was dry, and no sound came out. She swallowed, tried to form some saliva, swallowed again.

"Daddy," she croaked weakly and tried to sit up.

"Daddy," this time a bit louder.

"Daddy! Daddy, over here. I'm here....oh Daddy... oh God. Oh God. Thank you God. You sent my daddy!"

John spotted movement in the grass at about the same time he heard her voice. Yes! It was her. And she was alive. His Beth was alive. Yes, Yes, Yes. Oh God, thank you. Thank you. He was running and crying. She was sitting up, trying to get to her feet when he finally reached her. John knelt down to her and scooped her up in his arms effortlessly. She was his little girl again, and she was safe in his arms. He was sobbing into her hair.

"You're alive. You're alive. Do you know how much your mother and I have prayed to find you?"

"I'm sorry, Daddy. I'm so sorry. I messed up."

"Your mom and I know about the baby, honey. It's okay. Everything's okay now."

"The baby's gone," she sobbed. " I put him in the river before the storm. "He's gone..." Her voice trailed off in sorrow.

"The baby is fine, honey. He's fine. A couple found him in the canoe this morning and took him to the hospital. Your mom and I saw it on the morning news. We knew it had to be you. We just knew it. Oh, your mom is going to be so happy."

"What? My baby ... he's fine?"

"He's fine. But look at you. You need a hospital. Don't worry, baby. Daddy's going get you out of here."

John looked up to see Sheriff Wright and five other men come running down the hill towards them.

"I found her. I found my baby!" he shouted as they approached.

"Let's get you to the hospital young lady and get you checked out. You gave us all quite a scare."

"How did you find me?"

"The canoe. It had Catfish's name painted on the side. Catfish said you took off right before the storm hit."

289

"You *talkea* to him? Beth's eyes widened in fear.

"Only briefly. He's in bad shape in Perry County Medical. His truck went off the road during the storm."

"He's crazy. He wouldn't let me leave, Daddy. He killed her...he killed his wife." She was blubbering now.

"What did she say? Wait...Beth...what did you say about his wife," the sheriff asked.

"He killed her. I found her grave. It's around the bend. No telling what he did to her. Oh Daddy, get me out of here. Please get me out of here."

"We're going honey. We're going." He carried her as he walked back up the steep hill. "He won't hurt anyone else, honey."

"Catfish is going to jail for a very long time. If that is Inetha in that grave, then he faces murder charges along with federal drug trafficking. Not to mention theft of the Tut treasure. Beth, where did you get the box with the rings? Did they come from Catfish?"

"I found them hid in a closet with the truck keys. I tried to escape, but he caught me. I knocked him out with a beer bottle and ran."

"How in the thunder did an old river rat from Perry County

end up with the Tut treasure, I wonder."

"The Tut treasure?" said John.

"Yes, it was stolen in a robbery in Memphis back in January. Probably about the same time Beth disappeared."

"Memphis. That's where I was...I was in Memphis when he offered to drive me home. Oh God, if I had known. If I had only known..."

"It's okay, honey. We all make mistakes. Let's get you to your mama. And your son."

"Mama's here?"

"Yes. She's with Moses."

"Moses?"

"That's what the couple named him that found him, because they drew him out of the water."

"Moses," Beth repeated faintly as she collapsed in exhaustion on her daddy's shoulder.

Chapter 32

Trouble Brewin'

"What a precious bundle you are. Yes you are," cooed
Carolyn as she held the tiny newborn in her arms, rocking him back
and forth in the nursery's cherry wood rocker.

"We've got a lot of catching up to do with your mama. But I
promise you, you're going to be one spoiled little boy. Oh, I love
you so much already. Look how bright those eyes are. You're
listening to me, aren't you?"

Carolyn looked into the face of her grandchild. She stroked the
blonde fluff on his head and whispered to him about his future.
She did not hear the door open behind her. She only heard it slam
shut. Startled she looked up to see the charge nurse who was stiff
with fear as she was pushed into the nursery by a tall, thin patient
with a cast on his leg.

Carolyn was so shocked by the interruption that she stood up, holding the baby close to her chest to protect him. Her first thought was that a disoriented mental patient had gotten unruly. But then she caught the glint of metal in his hands. What appeared to be a pair of surgical scissors were opened and pointed toward the nurse. When the thin man spoke, his voice was gruff and sharp.

"Get over there woman. And don't make a sound. Don't make me cut your tongue out."

The nurse, though shaken, managed to get to crawl over to where Carolyn stood. Catfish's eyes narrowed.

"Don't go gettin' any ideas. You," he said nodding at Carolyn, "you sit back down nice and slow."

Carolyn hesitated for just a second too long.

"Now! Do as yer to told," he bellowed in a voice that was unnatural for such a small frame. The demon inside him had taken over.

Startled, she jumped and then nearly lost her balance backing toward the rocker. Her eyes darted around the room to find the nearest telephone, which she noted with disappointment, was directly behind Catfish on the wall near the exit.

293

"What...do you want..." began the nurse.

"I come for PJay. Give him to me," he ordered as he hobbled toward Carolyn -- the scissors in one hand, the other arm flailing out to his side for balance. She automatically covered the baby with her forearm.

"No. I won't."

The charge nurse was crouching on the floor at the foot of the rocker. At Carolyn's refusal, he grabbed the nurse by her auburn bob and yanked her to her feet one-handed. He held the scissors against her jugular.

"You will. Or she bleeds to death. You want that on yer conscience?"

Carolyn gasped. The nurse was mouthing the word, "no" silently to Carolyn. Did she mean no, don't let her bleed to death? Or no, don't give him the baby? There wasn't time to decipher the code. The nurse elbowed Catfish as hard as she could between his broken ribs. He howled in pain and doubled over, letting the scissors fall to the floor. She turned and shoved him with both hands as hard as she could back against the wall, then grabbed the scissors. He fell to his knees groaning.

Carolyn seized the opportunity to run for the door with the baby. She stopped with the door halfway open and called back.

"We have to get security. We have to make sure he doesn't leave this room. She could tell the nurse was having trouble deciding whether to finish him off or to help him up.

"My ribs...you punctured my lung..." Catfish was gasping for air in short, sharp puffs. "You aim to...to just...let me die? Fine nurse you are." The nurse drew the scissors up as if to stab him, a look of hatred burning in her angry eyes.

"Don't kill him. He knows where my Beth is. We need help."

Sheriff Dameron was on his way down the right wing toward the nurse's desk to inquire of Sheriff Wright when he heard the ruckus down the hall behind him. His keen sense of trouble kicked in, and he turned about face and went in the direction of the noise. When he heard a woman yelling, "Someone call Security...Quick...help!" he pulled his revolver and broke into a run down the long hall toward the nursery. He could see two women, and one appeared to be holding a baby. They were waving and yelling for him to hurry. The nurse was struggling to pull a heavy

295

office desk in front of the door to the nursery to keep Catfish

inside. Inside Catfish lay struggling for air -- knowing in his heart

that his reign over this kingdom was swiftly coming to an end.

"What is it?"

"Sheriff Dameron?" Carolyn blinked, a bit confused, and then

she realized he must be there to find Beth too. "That man tried to

kill us and take the baby," Carolyn explained. "He knows

something about Beth. Make him tell you where she is," she

pleaded.

"First, let's get him detained, ma'am. Then we'll get the

facts. Step back."

The sheriff leaned sideways to check out the nursery

through the viewing window. What he saw surprised him. Catfish

was lying on the floor clutching his heart. His eyes stared straight

ahead, his mouth agape, and his face was contorted in a most

unnatural shade of purple.

"I think we're too late for questions," he said glumly. "We

may never find her now."

Carolyn peered over his shoulder and let out a long wail of

grief. "No...no...noooo." She sobbed as she clung to the infant that had begun to squall loudly. Time stood still as all hope of finding her only child alive had just expired on the floor of Perry County Medical Center.

"God have mercy on that pitiful soul," was all the nurse could muster. But Carolyn knew in her heart that even if God somehow forgave him, she never would.

Chapter 33

Joy Unspeakable

It was early afternoon when the Sheriff's car carrying John and Beth approached Perry County Medical. The media had gathered on the parking lot and were in the process of setting up their cameras. There were vans from the three major networks, as well as CNN, FOX, and the Weather Channel.

"Aw man, I forgot about the press conference. This is gonna be a circus," Sheriff Wright remarked.

John pulled Elizabeth to him protectively.

"Don't look their way. They don't know that we've found you. Once they discover who's in the car, we'll never make it inside."

Sheriff Wright noticed the Madison County Sheriff's car in the parking lot. He reached for his cell phone, dialed the hospital, and asked for Sheriff Dameron.

"Glad you could make it. Rus Wright here. We've got the girl. We need you to run interference so we can get her into the ER and get her checked out."

"Good work, Sheriff. We've been quite busy ourselves. We've had a hostage situation in the nursery; the patient you brought in this morning fell over dead with a heart attack. Mrs. Merriweather believes this person was after the baby. I'm pretty sure he is involved in some way. Once we get Beth in here, we can see if she can identify him."

"He's dead? Well, that's going to throw a kink in the Tut investigation, but it will save the taxpayers his prison bill. He was facing multiple charges -- drug trafficking, kidnapping, felony theft, and possibly murder. There's an unmarked grave back on his property that we think might be his wife."

Sheriff Dameron let out a soft, low whistle. In all his years in law enforcement, he had never handled a case with so many federal charges against one perpetrator. The press was going to eat

299

this up.

"Drive around back to the cafeteria entrance. I'll send word that the conference is about to begin. That will buy you some time. A deputy will be there to bring you all to the room where we have Mrs. Merriweather and the baby."

Once he hung up the phone, Sheriff Dameron turned on his heel and headed for the private room where he had set up Mrs. Merriweather and her grandchild to shield them from the onslaught of publicity. A deputy stood guarding the doorway. The Sheriff whispered the good news to the deputy, who broke out in a huge grin and trotted off towards the cafeteria.

"Mrs. Merriweather. How are you and the baby? You two bouncing back okay?"

"I think we're going to be just fine."

"I think so too -- especially after you hear the good news."

Carolyn guessed the good news before the Sheriff could even get it out. She ran to him, arms outstretched, questioning.

"They found her! Is she okay?"

"They're bringing her in as we speak."

Carolyn's hand went to her heart. She was speechless. All

of those nights in anguish and fervent prayer. All of those grey winter days she had dreamed of her child coming home. And now it was happening. Beth was alive. Her baby was alive.

"Thank you God!" She shouted and nearly danced for joy. She grabbed the Sheriff, hugged him and was sobbing on his shoulder when the door opened behind him. The deputy stuck his head in to make sure everything was okay and then stepped aside. Beth was seated in a wheelchair with John standing behind her. Her hair was shorter than when Carolyn had seen her last, and it was dirty and stringy. Blood streaked the side of Beth's face from where she had struck her head on the rock. It stained the cotton housedress that was torn and ragged and revealed the cuts caked with dried blood on her legs. She looked like she had been through hell and back. But she was alive. Her only daughter was alive. Carolyn stood speechless for a half second.

"Mom," Beth said weakly. "Mom!"

Carolyn ran to the wheelchair sobbing. She bent to peer into her daughter's face. Yes, this was the baby she had grieved for all these months. This was her flesh and blood smiling up at her with tears streaking through the blood and mud. Her eyes were

301

older and wiser. But it was her Elizabeth. And she was safe. She wanted to grab her and hold her tightly and never let her out of her sight again, but seeing the condition she was in, she tenderly took Beth's face into her trembling hands and just knelt there staring, taking in the moment. Finally she found her voice.

"God brought you back to me. It's a miracle..."

"I know, Mom. I'm sorry for all the heartache I've caused."

"Honey, we love you. We love *both* of you." As if on cue, the infant began to cry.

"My baby! Oh God, thank you, God. Thank you!" Beth was crying hysterically as her mother went to the crib and gathered the baby up to take him to his mother. She laid the baby gently in Beth's arms, and Beth leaned down to kiss the baby's brow.

"I was so worried about you. I thought I had lost you forever. Oh God, I can't believe it. We're all here, together."

"Yes, and we're going to stay together this time, no matter what happens. Beth, your mom and I are here for you darling." John was choked with emotion as he knelt to take his first look at his grandson. He thought the baby resembled his side of the family, but then it might look more like a Daily.

"We've got to call Chris!"

"Dad..." Beth began, but the reunion was interrupted by a doctor entering the room.

"I hate to break up the reunion. But I think it's best we examine the patient and get her treated and get her some rest. It appears she's had quite the ordeal. If you would like, you can wait here, and I'll make sure she's brought back to this room."

Carolyn kissed her daughter on the head and stroked her hair gently. In eight short months her daughter had passed from girlhood to womanhood; the transformation was astounding. There was so much she wanted to know. So much she was afraid to ask. But she knew that no matter what, she would spend the rest of her days loving and caring for her daughter and this precious grandchild. There was no room in this mother's heart for judgment or criticism. No matter how much this ordeal had changed Beth, she was still her own flesh and blood. There was no condemnation. Her prodigal had returned.

As Beth was wheeled away, Carolyn looked down at the sweet smelling bundle in her arms. She pressed her cheek to his soft head. She knew if she was ever going to pick up the pieces of this trial and move on that she was going to have to do the unthinkable. Forgiving Beth was easy. But to ever have complete peace, she was going to have to search her heart. Somehow, some way, she was going to have to find it in her heart to forgive Catfish. Not for his sake. Unless he had made a dying confession to Christ, it was too late for him. But for her own sake, she must rid her heart of this bitter hatred she had held for him. She stared into the trusting eyes of the child, and in an instant her choice was made.

"Oh God," she breathed. "I need your help."

305

Chapter 34

A Slave No More

March 2007

Eight months later, Carolyn and John sat on a park bench

holding a chubby blonde haired boy dressed in a navy and white

sailor suit. The baby was holding the sailor cap up to his mouth

and gnawing on its brim, perfectly content to sit and watch the

crowds of people pass by on their way to get in line for the rides. A

luminous pale Luna moth hovered around the trio, flitting from the

hat to Carolyn's red shirt to John's shoulder. Dollywood was abuzz

with Spring Break activity, and the weather was as perfect a day as

you can get in the South this time of year. John leaned in to tickle the baby. He goosed him lightly between the ribs, and the baby squealed in delight.

"Look at him. Isn't he gorgeous." Carolyn gushed.

"A perfect specimen I'd say. A Luna moth isn't it?"

"I was talking about Moses. Our daughter makes handsome babies."

"Your son-in-law isn't too shabby either, I might add."

"I'll concede to that. My opinion of him has changed considerably over the last little bit."

"Well, it didn't hurt that he came to you first on Christmas Eve to ask her hand, either, did it?"

"Not a bit." He paused in reflection for a moment, and then continued. "I'm glad they saw things our way and decided to let us help them out while they go back to school."

"Me too. Since they let Beth keep the scholarships, she wants to do something else with the reward money for the King Tut treasure."

"Oh really? What's that?"

"She told me she wants to start a Christian home for unwed

307

mothers; she's going to call it 'Treasures from Heaven.' I think it's a great idea."

"Our Beth has grown up so much through all this. I can really see God working in her -- and Chris."

"You know how many times I questioned God about this whole ordeal, and I never once stopped to think about how it could be working together for good." Round and round above them a perfect circle was rotating high above the park.

Beth Daily could see her parents holding little Moses Daily below. She smiled and leaned into her new husband's shoulder. As the Ferris wheel began its ascent to the top, Beth held her breath at the beauty and wonder of God's perfect world displayed at every turn. God had created this world -- all of it. He created the mountains, the rivers, and even the wilderness. Chris took her hand and squeezed gently. And now that she had surrendered her life to Him, she was safe.

"What are you thinking about?" Chris asked.

"How blessed I am to have you and Moses. And how good God is."

"I know, Beth. I thought I'd never see you again. He's

answered so many prayers. You're free now. You're free."

Peace filled her heart, and a knowing smile crossed her face. The Lord had redeemed her and set her back on the path of righteousness and restored her joy. Not only had He made the three a family, but He'd given her an opportunity to help other girls in trouble as well.

The media had given her full credit for the recovery of the Tut treasure, but none of it compared to what God had done for her over the past year. Her amazing God had delivered her from sin, pride, and the bitter bondage of Pharaoh's hand, and she had come forth from the wilderness of that bleak Egypt, not only a woman, but a new creation—forever His and forever free.

THE END

NOTES